5-3PBC

SECOND TO NONE

The Roberto Alomar Story
with Stephen Brunt

VIKING

VIKING
Published by the Penguin Group
Penguin Books Canada Ltd, 10 Alcorn Avenue, Toronto, Ontario, Canada
M4V 3B2
Penguin Books Ltd, 27 Wrights Lane, London W8 5TZ, England
Viking Penguin, a division of Penguin Books USA Inc., 375 Hudson Street,
New York, New York 10014, USA
Penguin Books Australia Ltd, Ringwood, Victoria, Australia
Penguin Books (NZ) Ltd, 182-190 Wairau Road, Auckland 10, New Zealand

Penguin Books Ltd, Registered Offices: Harmondsworth, Middlesex, England

First published 1993

10 9 8 7 6 5 4 3 2 1

Printed and bound in Canada on acid free paper ∞

Canadian Cataloguing in Publication Data
Brunt, Stephen
    Second to none: the Roberto Alomar story

ISBN 0-670-84795-X

1. Alomar, Roberto. 2. Baseball players —
Canada — Biography. 3. Baseball players —
United States — Biography. I. Title.

GV865-A46B78 1992   796.357.092   C92-094679-8

To my family — and especially my mother.

RA

To Nat, Jake and Holly.

SB

◇ ACKNOWLEDGMENTS

This book could not have been written without the help of many people who — especially considering the unusual circumstances under which the project was undertaken — were invaluable in offering their time, their knowledge, and their enthusiasm.

The Alomar family — Sandy, Maria, Sandy Jr. and Sandia — welcomed me into their home in Salinas and told me the story of Roberto's childhood, as did Carmen Pabon, who graciously shared her memories. Their openness and warmth was greatly appreciated.

Also in Puerto Rico, Luis Rosa, the super scout, offered key insights into baseball on the island.

In Toronto, Betty John, Roberto's second mom, was a great help, as were Pat Gillick, Joe Carter and Cito Gaston. Also in the baseball world, thanks to Jack McKeon, Deacon Jones, Barry Bloom, Tony Gwynn and Larry Millson.

John Boggs, Roberto's agent, was a superb facilitator who helped to smooth the waters.

Steve Bright and Phil Andrews, computer masters extraordinaire from the University of Western Ontario Graduate School of Journalism, provided first-rate research material without which the book could not have been completed.

My thanks, especially, to the fine folks at Penguin who got me into this book and then helped get me through it, especially Cynthia Good, Jackie Kaiser, and freelance editor Greg Ioannou. It was a pleasure working with you again.

Two books — *Puerto Rico: A Political and Cultural History* by Arturo Morales Carrion and *Puerto Rico* edited by Chris Caldwell and Tad Ames — greatly enhanced my knowledge of Puerto Rican culture and history.

Finally, I'd like to thank my wife, Jeanie MacFarlane, as always my first and best editor, my sounding board and my friend, who survived these past months with patience, tolerance and mostly good humour, and who also managed to keep two rambunctious boys out of their father's hair and give birth to a perfect daughter along the way. I owe you one.

◇ CONTENTS

	Introduction	xi
1	The Game	1
2	Home	25
3	The Family Business	44
4	Learning the Ropes	63
5	Big Leaguer	83
6	Detour	99
7	Blue Jay	118
8	A Star is Born	137
9	Different Cast, Different Story	146
10	The Championship Season	156
11	The Fall Classic	175
12	The Best	191
	Epilogue	214

◇ INTRODUCTION

Three men conspire to draw a straight line. One pushes the cart, the wheels squeaking twice each revolution, laying down a white stripe of lime on the red-brown earth. A second man walks ahead, looking down, judging the angle with his eye, offering direction and guidance. The third merely supervises but he supervises well, with a grand, imperious authority. His t-shirt hikes up just above his navel.

Eventually, as the sun sets and the sky turns violet above Estadio Municipal Hiram Bithorn, the simultaneously 1950s-futuristic and 1990s-down-at-the-heels ballpark in central San Juan, they make their way from third to home and the line is strong enough and true enough to satisfy the boss. Now just one more to go and the game can start.

I am sitting in the stands in the middle of January, eating a taco, soaking up the sights and sounds as the umpires begin their slow stroll to the plate. Players from the Santurce Cangrejeros, the "Crabbers," who wear Dodger blue, and the San Juan Metros, who wear the colours of the New York Mets, stand and talk and play a little soft toss. Juan Gonzalez, the towering home run king of the Texas Rangers — known as "Igor" to all of Puerto Rico — climbs to the top of the dugout steps and is immediately swarmed by a crowd of young boys. They kneel on the top of the dugout in a row, bending over, bottoms to the crowd, holding cards and baseballs to be autographed. There are no security forces to clear them out, no ushers to shoo them back to their seats. On the scoreboard in straightaway centrefield, the lights have come on. "Bienvenidos Fanaticos," it reads.

The Puerto Rican winter league season is already near the end of the round-robin phase, when the top four teams in the six-team loop (this year, Santurce, San Juan, the Mayaguez Indians from the west coast and the Ponce Lions from the south) vie for a place in the best-of-seven championship series. The winner of that series will have the opportunity to compete for the coveted Caribbean title.

With three games to go, there is a virtual dead heat among the four teams, and so this game and every remaining game is critically important. In the stands on another perfect Caribbean night, the air is hot and thick, the sea breeze blowing hard, the crowd is divided into perfectly symmetrical halves. Both of these are home teams — Santurce is a San Juan suburb — and so the fanaticos are split like the crowd at a college football game. There are men and women, teenage lovers arm in arm, and especially there are children everywhere. Friends greet each other, touching hands, clasping shoulders, always making contact. The pina colada vendor pauses from his shouting to half embrace the chocolate vendor. A man with a conga and another with a cow bell climb to a high row. There they begin the rhythm that will punctuate the game, commenting on hits and errors, on moments of joy and tragedy alike, perfectly articulate.

Baseball came to Puerto Rico, as it did to the Dominican Republic and to Japan, courtesy of American invaders. In 1898, Teddy Roosevelt and the Yanks claimed the island where Christopher Columbus had landed about four hundred years earlier as a spoil of the short and decisive Spanish-American war. Today, the great Spanish fortresses built in the sixteenth century still dominate old San Juan, but otherwise the victors own the landscape, marking their territory with Burger Kings and Kentucky Fried Chickens and, of course, the ubiquitous golden arches. Their national pastime is now also the Puerto Rican national pastime, but here the natives have won a subtle victory, making the game truly their own. Baseball in San Juan is not like baseball in Dubuque. It has become part of the Indian/Spanish/African/American gumbo that is Puerto Rican culture, and it has been exported as the baseball heroes from this small island have gone afar to be counted among the very best in the world: the sainted Roberto Clemente, the great home-run hitter Orlando Cepeda, and now a host of young stars like Gonzales.

It is nearly time for the first pitch — in fact it was time for the first pitch ten minutes ago — but the little boy won't leave the field. He is perhaps eighteen months old, a mere "Pamper," as the locals say. He has wavy hair and big brown eyes and is decked out in a full white baseball uniform with his name — Luis — written across his tiny shoulders. In his hands he holds an orange plastic bat.

Maco Oliveras, the manager of the Cangrejeros, picks up a ball, drops down in a crouch, and offers to pitch to Luis. The boy holds the bat over his shoulder with one hand and stands facing Oliveras head on. This just won't do. Much of the crowd is watching and laughing now as Oliveras corrects the boy's stance, placing the bat on his shoulder, shifting his feet until they are parallel. Then, two hands on the bat, staring straight forward, and the final piece, a slight bend of the knees. Oliveras crouches and pitches and Luis, who now looks like Eddie Gaedel, the midget who batted once in the major leagues, stays as still as a statue, The ball goes by — the bat never moves — it hits the ground, and then Luis calmly walks to it, picks it up, and hands it back to Oliveras. He has the form down pat, but still the function eludes him.

The crowd is cheering and laughing. Luis for the first time notices his audience. He stares into the stands, but there's no fear in his eyes. Instead, he warms to his task, taking his stance again, bending his knees, waiting for the pitch, hearing his fans but focussing on the job at hand. Oliveras lobs another one and this time Luis takes a giant conceptual leap, swings the bat and sends the ball bouncing along the turf. Luis, exultant, lifts the bat in the air, pointing to the sky. As Oliveras holds him aloft and carries him back to his father's waiting arms, there is a long, loud round of applause. The little boy smiles a radiant smile as he disappears into the throng.

Then, and only then, is it time to play ball. The Metros win it 2–1 in ten innings.

Watching the game and, especially, watching the little boy, it strikes me that this same scene could have been played out fifteen or twenty years before. The stadium, the teams, the atmosphere have changed little, and there likely would have been another boy with curly, blondish hair, cafe au lait coloured skin and big, dark eyes, who was running around on the field with his older brother. He didn't have a uniform, except when he served as batboy, but he did have a father playing with the Cangrejeros. His dad was a local hero who had worked hard to make a career in the big leagues, who had been to an All Star Game and to the World Series.

Roberto Alomar carried his bat and glove everywhere, he cried if he got home from school too late to accompany his father to the park. When he did get on the field, even at the age of six or seven, he fielded grounders, shagged flyballs, turned double plays and played "pepper" with the men. When the game began, he would hang out in the clubhouse, or he would play ball with other kids beyond the outfield fence. Some of the others had talent, including his older brother Sandy, but Roberto was something special. His father's teammates saw a prodigy, already possessed with the instincts to play the game.

"There was something in the way he walked, the way he threw the ball, the way he hit, the way he behaved," Oliveras told me after the game. "You could tell that he was going to be a ballplayer."

Stephen Brunt
March 1993

SECOND
TO NONE

1

 THE GAME

It's called a high sky, so bright and clear and sapphire blue that when you stare into it, trying to find that little, round, white sphere, it seems it could have travelled all the way to the sun. Baseball in California on an October afternoon with not a cloud in sight can be like that: a joy for watching and tanning and eating popcorn and drinking beer, not such a joy for playing ball.

But who's complaining? Only four teams have the privilege, after all, of making it as far as 1992's Major League Baseball's championship round: the Atlanta Braves and Pittsburgh Pirates, Oakland Athletics and Toronto Blue Jays. Everyone else is already home relaxing, or is elsewhere preparing for another season that is still months away.

For instance, Sandy Alomar Jr., a catcher for the Cleveland Indians, is spending the afternoon in Ohio cleaning up his suburban home, and watching the pre-game show out of the corner of his eye, only half-listening to the announcers' babble. Sandy Alomar Sr., a minor league instructor with the Chicago Cubs, would normally have been in Mesa, Arizona, tutoring prospects at the club's training complex. Instead, since Mesa is not that far from Oakland, and since his son Roberto was one of the lucky few involved in the playoff, he has secured permission to play hookey for the weekend and catch games three, four and five of the American League Championship Series at the Oakland Coliseum.

The Coliseum is not one of the storied stadia in sports, not an antique jewel like Fenway Park or Wrigley Field, not a modern marvel like the SkyDome or a modern mock-jewel like Baltimore's Camden Yards. It is a big concrete donut that used to also play home to the Raiders of the National Football League, and since it is perched between an industrial area and a freeway, the vistas aren't going to remind anyone of Chavez Ravine.

But it is still a terrific place to watch a baseball game, especially on a day like this, and since it has been home to some of the best teams in modern baseball history, that ought to provide lore and legend enough. On a verdant field of real grass cut in a checkerboard pattern (although now, thanks to a recent Guns 'n' Roses concert, it is not quite as verdant as it might be), Reggie Jackson, Vida Blue, Joe Rudi, Charlie O., Dick Williams and all the rest worked their magic, Billyball briefly took the game by storm, Tony LaRussa, a lawyer by training, made managing sound like rocket science, and the Bash Brothers smacked forearms in celebration.

For devotees of the Toronto Blue Jays, one other memory of the place particularly holds sway: 1989, Our Boys versus Their Men, Rickey Henderson running wild, Dennis Eckersley wallowing in our humiliation, a second playoff in franchise history, a second exit short of the World Series — and it wasn't even close.

The Blue Jay believers figured with good reason it would be different in 1992. Oakland wasn't the same, Rickey wasn't the same, Jose Canseco had been consigned to Texas. These Blue Jays weren't those Blue Jays, not with Jack Morris and David Cone pitching, not with Joe Carter and Dave Winfield hitting, not with Roberto Alomar at second base. Even after Morris had lost game one at home, they had come back fighting to win the next two. Win this one, go up and it's just about over. The series might even end right here in Oakland, and then it would be on to The Show.

Sandy Alomar Sr. arrives at the park early, just like he always used to as a player, and takes a seat near the Blue Jays wives in the upper boxes. "I'm a real fan but I'm a quiet fan," he says. "I just like to stay quiet. My wife, she goes wild. But I'm different." Needless to say, he won't be one of the people waving a giant, blue foam letter "J" in celebration once the game starts. Just as he sits down, he catches the eye of one of the stadium ushers, a guy who has been around for as long as he has and who remembers Sandy from his playing days.

"Man," Sandy says, "you know we're going to finish it here. Two more wins and it's over."

"No way," says the usher, sporting a great big grin. "You guys ain't going to win."

Sandy played for fifteen years in the big leagues. He wasn't blessed with all of the talent in the world, so he had to fight to keep his job in baseball. Knowing more and working harder were his greatest assets. Now that both his sons have made it as well, it is pretty hard for him to watch the game for pure pleasure. It is especially hard because he sees baseball not as a spontaneous set of chance occurrences, but has learned to see it as the sum total of rights and wrongs — right decisions, wrong decisions, right positions, wrong positions, right attitudes, wrong attitudes.

If you think like that and see your baby boy lope onto the field to take infield practice before one of the most important games of his life, you wouldn't necessarily leap up and cheer. "I saw him taking infield and I didn't like the way he was doing it. I told him about it later. He was being too nonchalant. I said, 'If you're going to take infield like that, you might as well not even take it. Because that gives a bad impression of you. You know better than that. You know that we always talk about that. The way that you take infield, that's the way that you play the game.'"

In Salinas, Puerto Rico, everyone will watch the game. These Alomars are their Alomars, after all, favourite sons of this quiet little town on the south coast of the island. In the Monserrate neighbourhood, the attention will be particularly intense, especially at the white house with the white iron work where the small, yapping dogs pour out to greet every visitor. Maria Alomar and her daughter Sandia are a matched set — warm, shy, pretty, a little more emotive than the brothers, a lot more emotive than the father. For Maria, watching this game on television will be half unremitting joy, half unbearable ordeal. "I pray when it is on TV. I pray, 'Oh God, please help my son.'"

Her son is in the dugout, drawing two perfect black lines under his eyes, and then doing the same for his teammate, third baseman Kelly Gruber. There are all kinds of high tech sunglasses you can wear on the field these days. Eye black is prehistoric stuff by comparison, but it is also just what you would expect the ever-respectful baseball son of an idolized baseball father to use. It is the right way to battle a high sky in California on an October afternoon — even though, before the game is done, Robbie will have donned the shades as well.

The Athletics take the field, and the crowd shakes itself out of its sunny-day stupor to roar. You don't have to be a savant to rhyme off the Blue Jays lineup without looking at the scoreboard. When Cito Gaston finds something he likes, he sticks with it: Devon White, Roberto Alomar, Joe Carter, Dave Winfield, John Olerud, Candy Maldonado, Kelly Gruber, Pat Borders, Manuel Lee. The champions of the American League East.

Bob Welch (fifteen years in the majors, 199 career victories and a heroic battle with alcoholism) is Oakland's starter in game four. LaRussa has decided to go with a four-man rotation, while Gaston will be bringing back his game one starter. Morris, the money pitcher, was paid big dollars as a free agent during the off-season to win games just like this one. He couldn't save the day in game one, but now, as the stakes get higher, Morris figures to get better. Just remember what he did for Minnesota last year.

White steps up to lead off the game and strikes out, looking, on a forkball. He doesn't like the call by home plate umpire Durwood Merrill. While that's going on, Alomar, in the on-deck circle, sizes up what he is about to face. He has handled Welch easily during his career, hitting .385, and he is off to a decent start in the ALCS, 3–12, with a home run during the Jays victory in game three.

"When Welch is pitching, I always look for the ball. It all depends on how he's working me in the first at-bat. In this game, he tried something different every time I was at the plate."

Welch begins with a fastball, which Alomar fouls off for strike one. Then catcher Terry Steinbach sets up on the outside corner and Welch hits the target. Alomar takes the pitch for strike two. The next pitch is nearly the same pitch, but perhaps two inches off the plate. Alomar's eye tells his brain to tell his arms and hips and wrists to let it pass. "Then he threw me a change-up. I was just trying to make contact." It is a soft line drive single to leftfield, the opposite field. Rickey Henderson scoops it up as Alomar makes the turn at first.

His job changes now from hitter to base-stealer, a role at which he excels. It is partially a matter of simple foot speed, of course, but it's just as much a matter of using your eyes, of understanding and analyzing the pitching motion, of anticipating the pitcher's and catcher's actions, of committing to the steal at just the right moment, of exploding at the start and sliding to the part of the bag where you're least likely to be tagged. Alomar has studied all of those elements long and carefully with his father — a fine baserunner in his time — as tutor.

"When you're on first trying to steal, you have to watch the pitcher's feet and you have to watch his shoulders, whether he's opening up. If he opens up, when he starts to move in towards the plate he can't go back. You look at his legs too, even his head sometimes. You look at the catcher, just noting what kind of catcher is back there. You have to consider who's hitting and what the count is. You have to notice whether the pitcher has a high leg kick, and whether he's quick to home plate. Sometimes, the coach on first base will have a stop watch, and he can tell you how quick he is throwing over to first base. Other times, you pick up something in a pitcher's delivery that tells you when he's going home. If you spot that, you tell the coaches and they write it down.

"My Dad taught me a lot about stealing. You don't have to be fast to steal; you have to know how to steal. Some catchers you can't really run on, because they're pretty good throwers — Ivan Rodriguez, Sandy, Ron Karkovice. I can't tell you which pitchers have the best move to first, because that would give it away, but I will tell you that Charlie Hough might be the toughest one for me to steal on. He's real quick."

Welch has a high leg kick, and is slow to the plate. The catcher, Terry Steinbach, has a good arm and a quick release. To compensate for his delivery, Welch throws over to first often, he varies his move, and he comes perilously close to balking by not reaching the required full stop before he goes to the plate.

At bat is Joe Carter, Alomar's best friend on the team, one of the game's most consistent run producers, a great professional hitter. Before Carter sees a pitch, Welch throws to first, though not hard, and Alomar is back standing up. Alomar takes his lead again, his eyes fixed on Welch, trying to decipher each movement.

Welch steps and delivers. Carter takes a fastball. Ball one. Welch throws to first again, and again. Alomar easily makes the bag. Then the pitch goes to Carter, who fouls it off: 1–1.

Alomar is running on the next pitch. He breaks for second. It is a strike, and Steinbach is up quickly with the ball. Alomar aborts the steal a third of the way to second and scurries back. Steinbach throws behind him to first. Mark McGwire fields the throw and sweeps his glove over the base. Alomar's hand just avoids him. He clutches a corner of the bag. Safe, but close.

"Sometimes you try and bluff to see if there will be a pitch out. You try and play with their minds. As soon as you go, you can look and see if the catcher is moving real quick to the outside corner, and you have time to go back. That wasn't really a bluff, though. I was going to go. But I saw the pitch out, so I stayed."

Carter takes a ball, and turns to Merrill. Alomar turns to talk to the first base umpire.

"After that pitch, I asked Joe Brinkman if he balked. You cannot bend your knee and throw to first. It should have been a balk. And sometimes he wasn't stopping in his motion. Joe Carter was telling the home plate umpire the same thing: 'Make him stop. Make him stop.' When I told Brinkman, he said 'This is the 1990s.' I told him, 'A balk in the 90s is still a balk, because he still has to stop.' Maybe after that he got a little mad at me."

Alomar is ready to steal on the next pitch. He is leaning towards second. Welch begins his motion, then throws quickly to first. Alomar tries to shift his weight back towards the base. He grabs for the bag as McGwire sweeps with the tag. Replays will later make it appear that McGwire misses Alomar's shoulder as he gets back safely. But Brinkman calls him out, with a little theatrical flourish.

In disbelief, Alomar jumps to his feet and starts to argue the call. He holds his hands up in disgust. Gaston, wearing a pair of high tech reflective shades, rushes out of the dugout to put himself between the umpire and his player. If anyone is going to get tossed it will be him, and since Brinkman is viewed as a long-time antagonist of the Blue Jays, you never know.

"I told him I was safe. Cito came out, and Brinkman told him that he thought I was out. I just walked off the field and didn't let that bug me. I just played my game."

Gaston cuts his argument short, and then Carter pops up to end the inning. The As step up against Jack Morris, and despite an error by Lee that puts leadoff man Rickey Henderson on second, the Jays escape unscathed. In the top of the second, John Olerud launches a solo home run to left, and the Blue Jays lead 1–0.

The As go quietly in the bottom of the second, and the Jays come to bat in the third. With one out, Lee singles. White strikes out. Alomar faces Welch for the second time and is presented with a different pitching pattern. First comes a high fastball out of the strike zone for ball one. "Sometimes you have to let the pitcher pitch to you so you can see a few things. Plus I took a pitch for Lee. On the second pitch, I put my bat a little in front of the catcher's face, so he wouldn't have good vision if Manny tries to steal." The pitch is a ball, as is the next, a fastball outside. "Then on 3–0, he threw me a fastball right over the middle of the plate." Alomar takes it for strike one. "I kind of knew he wasn't going to throw me my pitch. He was going to throw me his pitch. He did. He threw me a change-up, a little bit high. I was looking for a fastball, for something inside, so I could drive it." The change-up misses the strike zone, and Alomar walks. Both he and Lee are stranded when Carter flies out.

Morris returns to face the As in the bottom of the third. He has looked strong early in the game. His velocity is fine, but now his control begins to desert him. Pitching from behind, he is far less effective. Mike Bordick leads off with a single. Lance Blankenship singles on a 3–2 pitch. Henderson hits a bloop single and Bordick scores. It's 1–1. Ruben Sierra hits a sacrifice fly. It's 2–1 Oakland. Harold Baines doubles down the rightfield line, and it's 3–1. Morris walks home run king Mark McGwire intentionally, and then walks Steinbach unintentionally to force in the fourth Oakland run. Then Carney Lansford bangs the ball into the dirt in front of home plate. It scoots past Morris and dribbles to the shortstop. Everyone is safe. It's 5–1.

Bordick comes to the plate again with one out, the As having batted around. He hits a groundball to Lee that is slowed by the infield grass. Lee scoops it up then relays it to Alomar, who completes the double play to end the inning.

It's a routine play, 6–4–3 on the scorecards. But in this game at this moment, it's also a crucial rally killer. One mistake, one miscalculation, and the inning continues. Instead, two players working in harmony flawlessly carry out the most complex series of thoughts and movements in the game of baseball. It is made to look easy, but it isn't.

"Making the double play is one of the toughest plays for a second baseman because you don't see the runner coming," Alomar says. "You have to know if the runner has good speed, and you have to know who is running from home plate, too. That changes where you take the ball from the shortstop. You want to stay behind the base, so you can protect yourself from the sliding runner and not get hurt. You like to know where the throw is coming. That's why you need to have good communication with the shortstop. A bad throw can surprise you. I'll tell my guy to give me the ball behind the base, or sometimes in front of the base. It depends who you're playing against. With a team that doesn't have much speed, you can take it a little easier.

"You tell the guy to throw to your right hand or your right shoulder. You have to catch the ball, and then just as soon as you catch it you have to throw it. So if you caught the ball at your left shoulder, you would have to bring it all the way back to your right shoulder to throw it. That gives the runner a few more seconds.

"At the same time as you catch the ball, you're pivoting on your left leg. My foot is landing on top of the bag when I catch the ball, then I go to the back of the bag as I make the throw. So the runner has to slide over the bag to get to me. At least it slows him down."

The Jays accomplish nothing in the top of the fourth, then stumble through the bottom of the inning, though they eventually get out of it unscathed. Morris doesn't survive it though. With one out and two on, Gaston decides he has seen enough, yanking Morris and bringing in Todd Stottlemyre.

"Really, Morris pitched a pretty good game," Alomar says. "In the post-season, he just seemed to always make one crucial mistake, like the home run by Harold Baines in game one of the ALCS. In this game, he just didn't have the control. But he's the kind of guy who goes out there and competes. He always tries his best. A lot of what happened in this game were rollers and bloopers, plus his control problem. But he stays in the game and keeps trying."

In the top of the fifth, there are two out when White beats out an infield hit, bringing Alomar to the plate for the third time in the game. "There was a man on base, so Welch pitched to me a little different. I hit his change-up in my first at-bat. The time before he had tried to get me out with a fastball outside. This time I figured he was going to try and keep the ball outside because Devon was on first base, and he didn't want me to pull it. I didn't think Devo was going to run, because we were down 5–1. He threw me another fastball outside, and then a curveball on the inside part of the plate — he threw me one for a ball in the first at-bat. I was looking for something on the inside of the plate, because with Devo being held on by the baseman the hole was open between first and second. On the next pitch, the ball was an outside strike and I just went with it."

Alomar drives a single up the middle. White goes to third, but Carter flies out to end the inning.

Welch is cruising now. LaRussa had hoped to get five decent innings out of him, but it appears in quality and quantity he's going to get much more than that. The As score another run in the sixth to go up 6–1, and in the top of the seventh Welch looks better than ever. He's ahead and he's throwing strikes — sixteen of twenty-one pitches at one point — as he strikes out Lee and White to finish the Jays with a flourish. That makes seven Ks for Welch, his high-water mark in an injury-plagued season. On the other side, Toronto has hurt its own cause by committing four errors.

The Jays now have six outs left, they trail by five runs, and across North America, viewers are losing interest, flipping to whatever football game is still in progress. The announcers start mining for trivia to explain just how unlikely a Blue Jays comeback would be: in the long history of baseball, no team has ever trailed a post-season game by five or more runs after seven innings and come back to win; the As had blown a lead of five or more runs just once in the 162-game regular season; the Jays of 1992 aren't a great comeback team. There is also the small matter of the fellow just now feeling his adrenalin surge down in the Oakland bullpen. Black eyes and moustache, hair billowing out from under his cap, all business, pretty near perfection: Dennis Eckersley with a lead in the late innings is the baseball equivalent of money in the bank.

But at least the Toronto pen isn't making matters worse. The As don't do any damage in the bottom of the seventh, bringing Alomar to the plate to lead off the eighth. So far, he's won the mental battle with Welch, has outguessed him, figured out his pattern and anticipated his pitch. They are matched once more, each one knowing what has gone before, each one trying to guess what the other is thinking, to be one step ahead.

"I knew he was going to try to get me inside this time, because he had already thrown me two pitches outside and I got two hits on the outside corner. He started with a fastball inside for a strike, then he threw a ball outside. After that he throws me a fastball inside for strike two. I was taking that pitch, and they called it a strike. I thought it was a bit inside and I asked the umpire. He says, No, it was right there. That was okay. Now I could see for sure how he was going to pitch me. He threw me another fastball inside, but this time I was looking for the pitch. I just missed it and fouled it off. At 2–2, he tried to fool me — he threw a change-up outside. The catcher set up inside as a decoy and he saw that I wasn't ready for the pitch. But I still thought he was going to come back inside."

The next pitch is a fastball, high, inside, maybe out of the strike zone.

"That's the one I was looking for. It wasn't that much out of the strike zone. It was just a little high. Sometimes if you get on top of the ball when the pitch is high, you can hit it good."

Alomar tomahawks the ball into rightfield, leaping head first into second base with a double. Immediately

LaRussa heads for the mound. It's not hard to understand his thinking. Welch had finished the last inning exceptionally strongly. Even though he'd already far exceeded expectations, it was certainly worth letting him continue with a five-run lead. Maybe he'd get through another inning, saving the bullpen, and then he could bring in Eckersley to mop up in the ninth.

But now, Carter, Winfield and Olerud are coming. There's a man on and there's no reason to mess around. Welch is sent to the showers to a huge ovation from the Oakland partisans.

For the Blue Jays, it is the first time in a long time that they sense the game might be turning their way. Their nemesis is gone, replaced by reliever Jeff Parrett.

A run or two isn't going to make any difference for the Blue Jays. They need a sustained rally, they need men on base when the heart of the order comes to the plate. It's time to play a little conservatively. You can't afford to give up outs on the basepaths. Alomar knows that better than most — his father would have pounded the commandment into his head again and again since childhood. But he also knows that sometimes in baseball, as in life, rules are made to be broken.

"Normally, down 6–1, I wouldn't try to steal. But when he gives me the base, I have to take it. And I know that when I try to steal, Joe won't swing the bat. He'll let me steal the base. Parrett came in and he wasn't paying any attention to me. So I decided to go on the third pitch. I knew Joe was struggling a bit, and I wanted to make something happen. It's easier to steal third base than second base, even though it's a shorter throw for the catcher. Sometimes pitchers don't pay that much attention to you, they don't expect it, and you can get a good jump."

He gets an enormous jump. Steinbach's throw isn't close.

"I was on third and he had to pitch differently to Joe. He had to throw fastballs. All Joe had to do was hit a groundball and I could score."

Parrett goes to 3–0 on Carter, works back to a full count, and then gives up a single, scoring Alomar and making it 6–2. LaRussa calls the bullpen and tells the coach to get Eckersley warmed up. He's not going to mess around today. He needs to nail down this win. He needs to pull even in the series. It's a little early for Eck — normally he is a one-inning pitcher — but this is the playoffs; this is the difference between being tied 2–2 or down 3–1.

Winfield singles to left. Henderson makes a great play to cut off the ball, then wheels and throws to third in one motion. The ball reaches the base before Carter does, but Lansford doesn't get the tag down in time. The play becomes just another of the game's many "what-ifs."

Blue Jays at first and third, As up by four, nobody out. LaRussa walks to the mound — Parrett's gone, Eckersley's in, the crowd roars. On the Oakland bench, any tension is cut by the fact that Eckersley just doesn't blow saves.

"You know you're going to see Eckersley eventually," Alomar says. "I never thought we would see him that early, though. He's a great pitcher. You have to be really aggressive against him. You can't let him get on top of you. That day, I think his fastball was a little flat. It wasn't sinking like it usually does. When he's got his fastball moving to the outside corner, it's hard to hit because it's moving away from you. And then he's got the hard slider coming in to lefties. But he didn't have it that day."

Olerud comes to the plate. He has had a spectacular day already — a home run and a double in three trips to the plate. Eckersley serves up a fastball over the centre of the plate, and Olerud slaps it up the middle. Carter scores; it is 6–3. Candy Maldonado follows. Again Eckersley's first pitch is fat and inviting. Again it is rocketed to the outfield for a single.

It's 6–4. Suddenly the charge in the air is different. Eckersley can't intimidate anyone now. He is clearly mortal on this afternoon. There are two men on, nobody out, and the margin is only two.

Kelly Gruber comes up to bat. He swings at the first pitch — why not? — and just misses it, fouling it back. Then he hits a shallow liner to centrefield. Willie Wilson, battling the sun, slides to make a great catch. Pat Borders follows. He grounds weakly to second, advancing the runners to second and third. A single can tie the game. Gaston calls Lee, the number nine hitter, back to the dugout. He sends up Ed Sprague to pinch hit. Sprague, a third baseman/catcher, had a hit off Eckersley in game one of the ALCS, and he'll make his presence known again before the post-season is done.

Eckersley changes his pattern, getting ahead in the count with his curveball. The payoff pitch is a fastball, though, high in the strike zone. Sprague swings right through it and strikes out to end the inning.

What a relief for the As, what a relief for the crowd. Eckersley, who knows he has fought back off the ropes, swings his fist into the air and screams. Then he stares his most penetrating, evil stare at the Toronto dugout, and says something that the better lip readers in the television audience can make out. On the Toronto bench, they hear it clear as a bell.

"Of course we noticed," Alomar says. "It was the part of the emotion of the game and that moment. He thought that he had stopped the bleeding. He was staring into the Blue Jays dugout and he said something and that's when everybody got mad."

There is also some history to this. In the 1989 ALCS, while the As were burying the Jays, Toronto manager Cito Gaston, in a desperate moment, accused Eckersley of doctoring the baseball. The two had a ferocious on-field screaming match, with Eckersley saying something that made Gaston as publicly emotional as he had ever been. The veteran Jays, at least, remembered all that, so when Eckersley made his suggestion, they responded in kind. "If you had had a microphone in the dugout then," Joe Carter says, "all it would have picked up were bleeps."

When all the shouting stops, though, the situation remains the same. Entering the top of the ninth inning, Oakland fans don't have much cause for worry. Eckersley had his rocky moments, but now he appears to be back in form. He needs three more outs and has a two-run lead — a comfortable cushion for the best closer in baseball.

The announcers again start hauling out their stats: the As were 65–4 when Eckersley pitched: they were 81–1 carrying a lead into the ninth inning, with the only loss coming in a meaningless game during the last weekend of the season. And there is also the distinct possibility that the As might widen the margin. It is the bottom of the eighth, and they have runners on first and third with one out against Mike Timlin. Willie Wilson then hits a groundball to Alfredo Griffin, who has replaced Lee at shortstop. He fields it, realizes that he doesn't have a chance to turn the double play, then sees that Lance Blankenship, the runner on third, has wandered halfway to home plate. He fires the ball to Borders, and Blankenship is caught in a rundown. Ruben Sierra then strikes out swinging to end the threat.

The Blue Jays are left to hope for the miraculous. Still, it is Eck, it is two runs, and that's nearly always a fatal combination.

"In the ninth inning, Eckersley's going to go one, two, three and the game is over," the friendly usher says, teasing Sandy.

"Uh uh," Sandy says, talking more with his Alomar heart than his baseball head. "One, two, three and the ball is out of here. You'll see."

Devon White leads off the inning. "That was a big at-bat," Roberto Alomar says. "If he got on base, he could have made things happen. He went to a 3–2 count. Eckersley knew he couldn't walk him. Devon battled. He hit a few foul balls and then he got a hit." His line drive is sinking fast in leftfield. Henderson doesn't get a quick read on the ball. For just a second he is undecided — should he charge and try and make the catch, should he concede the single and play it safe, picking the ball up on the bounce? He decides to try and do something great and instead does something awful. He misses the ball, and it bounces past him all the way to the outfield fence. White winds up on third. Roberto Alomar takes his place in the batter's box.

"To be honest, I was vacuuming my carpet in Cleveland and I wasn't really paying that much attention to the game, because it was 6–1," Sandy Jr. says. "I remember watching Eckersley blowing people out. And then the announcer said the tying run is at the plate, Roberto Alomar. So then I started paying attention."

"I was praying watching it on the TV," Maria says. "'Oh God, please help my son.' I said, 'Maybe a home run?' Then naah. 'Maybe a hit?' I felt that Robbie could make something — maybe not a home run, but a base hit."

"I was trying to get Devo home and get on base any way I could," Alomar says. "I knew Joe Carter was coming up behind me. If I could get on base, we had a chance to tie the game. If I get on first, then I can try and steal second, and Joe could drive me home. I knew Eckersley wasn't going to pitch the same way to me. He wasn't going to leave the ball out there over the plate. So the first pitch he threw me a fastball outside for a ball. The second pitch he threw another fastball on the outside corner for a strike. I just wanted to see how he was going to pitch to me. After that he threw me a fastball inside, and I took it for a ball.

"He stayed away with the next pitch, another fastball, and I hit a line drive foul down the leftfield line. I just missed it. It was maybe five feet foul. That meant I had two strikes on me, so I had to concentrate on just making contact. I was thinking about a pitch inside. If he threw one outside, I'd just try and slap it to the opposite field. All I knew for sure was that I wasn't going to let him strike me out.

"He threw me a fastball inside and I took it. Then he threw me a slider and I fouled it off. The next pitch was a fastball in the middle of the plate. Maybe he was trying to throw me inside, because the pitch two pitches before was way in. He wanted to throw the same pitch but he got a little more of the plate. I was sitting on that pitch. I was waiting for it. You have to make up your mind in those situations — if he's going to throw you a pitch inside, you want to try and hit it hard. You have to focus on one pitch against a pitcher like Eckersley.

He's not the kind of guy who's going to go here and there. He's going to go after you.

"It really wasn't a big swing. It was just a swing to protect the plate. But as soon as I hit it, I knew it was gone. I put my hands up. It was a great feeling. It was a tie, and we never felt we could tie that game when it was 6–1. We never thought we could tie the game against the best pitcher in baseball. To hit a home run and tie the game in the ninth in the American League Championship Series — well, you would put your hands up, too."

Standing in the on-deck circle, Carter sees the swing, hears the crack of the ball off the bat.

"When Robbie hit it, he knew it was out right away. He threw up his arms. But I wasn't so sure. I was saying to myself, 'You'd better run it out, Robbie, you'd better run. Run, run.' And then I saw it going out. When he was coming around those bases my heart was pumping."

"I knew that if he made a mistake, Roberto would make him pay for it," Cito Gaston says. "I think that home run turned everything around."

In Salinas, Maria's prayers were answered.

"When I saw that home run, I died. I felt like I was in the air. I was running. And my daughter . . . aaaah! Everybody was crying. That was the most important game. If they lost that game, maybe they wouldn't go to the World Series. But you know, I did feel bad for the other guy, Eckersley. Oh, poor guy. I imagined that. I thought, 'I feel sorry for you, but that was my son who hit the home run.'"

In Cleveland, the vacuuming stopped.

"When I saw Robbie hit the ball and raise his arms, I got the chills," Sandy Jr. says. "I said, 'Wow, what happened?' The announcers said it was a tie ballgame, that Roberto Alomar's home run had tied the game. Here's my little brother going deep to tie a game in the play-offs. It's amazing."

In the stands, the small section of Blue Jay rooters were an island of ecstasy in a sea of trepidation. Sandy was elated, too, but in a very Sandy kind of way.

"I didn't like it when Roberto put his hands up. But that's the way the game is played now. Eckersley did it in the eighth inning when he struck out a kid. That's why some of the players got mad. But he has been doing that a lot. He was a gentleman after Robbie hit that homer. He accepted it. It's just part of the game. Robbie wasn't really showing Eckersley up. He was just showing his emotion. That's probably the biggest homer he ever hit in his life.

"After the home run, the usher got sore and he left. He left while we were cheering."

As Alomar rounds the bases, his teammates leave the bench to greet him. He leaps high and comes down with two feet on the plate. There are high fives all around, and there is lots of yelling at Eckersley, who tries to pull himself together and get through the inning. He gets Carter to fly out, Winfield to ground out. But Olerud comes up with yet another hit, a single, and Eckersley is pulled from the game. You could spend a lot of years watching a lot of ballgames and never see that sight again.

The Jays almost move ahead right there and then, as reliever Jim Corsi walks the bases full before inducing Borders to ground out. The game is tied and it's the bottom of the ninth.

Duane Ward comes in to pitch for Toronto. Unlike Oakland, the Jays have the luxury of carrying two great relief pitchers on their staff. Still in the bullpen is Tom Henke, who Gaston will use only if Toronto takes the lead.

The first batter, Baines, hits a groundball that Alomar fields running full bore to his right. He turns in the air to throw to first, where Carter has moved in place of Olerud, who was lifted for pinch runner Derek Bell. Carter can't scoop up the throw. Baines is then removed for a runner — Eric Fox, a 29-year-old rookie who had kicked around the minor leagues since 1986. He has some power and he has some wheels. With Mark McGwire at the plate, he gets a great jump on Ward, and steals second without drawing a throw.

A strange thing happens then. The game's greatest power hitter, who has been on the ball all series long, drops down a sacrifice bunt — a perfect sacrifice bunt that crawls along the first-base line. Fox goes to third with just one out, where he can score on a fly to the outfield, and where he might score on a groundball. Gaston has the choice of walking the bases loaded and going for the double play or bringing his infield in and trying to cut off the run at the plate. The slow grass might make it difficult to get two. He pulls everyone in, and has Ward pitch to the next batter, Steinbach. On an 0–1 pitch, Steinbach hits a groundball to the right side of the infield.

Alomar says, "I was playing way in. Steinbach hit the ball right at me. As soon as he made contact, I saw Fox go. Out of the corner of my eye, I could see him moving. When I caught the ball he was halfway between home plate and third base. I don't know why he went. Maybe it was his instincts. He went without anyone telling him to go. I would have stayed. If it's a high hop or a flyball, that's the only way you can score. You have to make sure the ball goes through. He probably thought it was a big hop, but we're playing on grass, not artificial turf. If it's a flyball, the coach can tell you to stop, but if it's a groundball it's your decision."

The play at the plate isn't even close. Easy out. The next batter, Lansford, grounds out, and the As lose their last real chance to win the game — and the series.

White singles for the Jays with one out in the tenth, and then for the first time in the game, the As manage to retire Alomar — he hits a line drive right at the shortstop. Carter singles, but Winfield pops out, and the game remains tied. Ward mows down the As in order in the bottom of the inning.

Derek Bell leads off the eleventh against reliever Kelly Downs. It is his first ever post-season at-bat, and it is a brilliant, tenacious piece of hitting. After working Downs to a full count, he fouls off three pitches in a row, before taking ball four, just out of the strike zone. That sets the stage. With a good baserunner on first, Downs' attention is divided. Candy Maldonado, the next hitter, slices a soft liner to right that Sierra seems to lose in the sun. It drops, finally, just inside the right-field line. There are runners at first and third with nobody out. Gruber follows and hits a line drive just inside first base. McGwire stretches out and makes a great, diving catch. It looks like a game-saver. A double play could get the As out of trouble now. But instead, Pat Borders hits a line drive into leftfield. Henderson makes the catch, but his throw doesn't come close to nailing Bell, who has tagged at third.

The improbable comeback is just about complete. The Blue Jays lead 7–6. In the bullpen, the Terminator begins to warm up.

They can do no further damage before the As come to bat in the bottom of the eleventh. Henke is coming off another great season, but at times he has looked like a different pitcher than in the past. The forkball as much as the fastball has been his payoff pitch.

Wilson, the leadoff hitter, flies out to left. Sierra follows with a single. The tying run is on base. Fox, the base-running goat of the bottom of the ninth, comes up with a chance to redeem himself and write a poetic ending to the game from an Oakland point of view. He can't do it, lofting a harmless fly to centre.

There is one out left, and mighty Casey comes to bat. McGwire is only 2–18 against Henke, but he's already had one home run and a bunch of near misses in the series. Of all the hitters in the game, he might be the one you'd most like to have at the plate if you needed a home run to win.

He fouls Henke's first pitch, a fastball, straight back. It is a great swing, a near miss, but it is also strike one. He pulls the next pitch hard and just foul down the left-field line. Strike two. The next pitch is popped straight back into the crowd.

And then Henke delivers a forkball, and McGwire reaches down in the strike zone to get it. It rises in a high arc, and for just a moment the optimists in the crowd think their dreams have come true. But then they see White standing in the outfield, looking up, not moving. The ball drops harmlessly into his glove.

"The game was over. We did it. The guys were real happy because we were only one win away." The celebration begins in Toronto, in Salinas, in Cleveland, in one happy section of the stands.

For the kid who never wanted to be anything but a ballplayer, whose fantasies were always about hitting the home run that wins a championship, no moment had ever been as sweet.

"That was the best game I ever played in my entire life in baseball."

2

 HOME

Behind the house where Maria Velasquez grew up there was a field, more a pasture than anything else, a place where the local boys came for softball after school. They would play and the girls would watch, and it was there one afternoon that Maria, who was twelve years old, first noticed the young man she would marry.

Santos Conde Alomar, called Sandy, was a year older than Maria. He was strong and serious and he said very little. The Alomar and Velasquez families lived a block and a half apart in Guayama, a small town on the south coast of Puerto Rico. It is a tranquil, simple place. Jobos Bay is sapphire blue and perfect, the climate is warm and dry. The people speak Spanish with their own regional accent. Once the sea and the sugar cane fields were the source of any wealth, though now many of the farms are gone.

San Juan is only forty miles away, across the great, green mountains, but the two places seem much farther apart — they must have seemed even more so in the days before a freeway cut through the Cordillera, making what was an arduous journey along twisting narrow roads quick and simple. The capital is loud and fast, alive with the sights and sounds of the island's culture. It is almost a seamless mix — Spanish, American, African, even a little indigenous aboriginal flavour from the island's original inhabitants, long ago assimilated into the melting pot, leaving their petroglyphs and ceremonial ball courts behind. The Taino tribe first made the maracas, the guiros, the Puerto Rican expatriates in New York City combined their sound with big band music to make salsa, which returned home and became the heartbeat of the island. In San Juan, you can dance to it 'til dawn.

There is dancing in Guayama, too, but life there, today as it was thirty years ago, moves at a more gentle pace. The courtship between a shy young girl and a shy young man lasted six and a half years.

"We talked. We went dancing, I liked him because he was quiet and he was shy," Maria remembers. "He studied at the same school as me, we studied together. I enjoyed being with him. He was a good young guy. He played basketball, he played everything and he was good at everything. Sports was his life. But what he really enjoyed was baseball. Baseball all the time."

Santos Alomar's family originally came from Ponce, the largest city on the south coast. His father drove a tractor in the sugar-cane fields. "There has always been a family tradition of baseball," he says. "My mother had some cousins who used to play and my father had some baseball talent, too. Our whole family has always been in baseball." Three of his brothers signed professional contracts with major league teams in the United States — Rafael with the Giants, Tony with the Cardinals,

Demetrio with the Kansas City Athletics. None of them made it to the big leagues. Sandy was the baby in the family.

"When I was a kid, they had Roberto Clemente and they had Vic Power. They had Orlando Cepeda, Luis Olmo, Juan Pizarro, Jose Santiago, Luis Arroyo. They didn't get as much publicity as they get now, but we had a lot of good players. I looked up to my brothers, but after them Cepeda was my favourite player. He used to help the young Puerto Rican kids in the States a lot; he used to take care of the kids.

"I played in little league, and then I went over and played in the Pony League in San Juan. Some of the guys over there saw me and thought that I had a lot of ability. Luis Olmo was a scout for the Milwaukee Braves then. They gave me a tryout and liked what they saw. I could run pretty good. I had a pretty decent arm. I used to swing the bat good. I was a little bit raw but I was the kind of guy who would retain whatever was told to me and put it into practice."

Sandy signed with the Braves in 1960 for a $12,000 bonus — a decent sum of money at the time for a 16-year-old shortstop who still had a lot to learn. "Because I was still in school, they sent me to play in Wellsville, N.Y., where my brother Demetrio was, for my two-month school vacation. In 1961, I spent the summer in Davenport, Iowa. My brother was there, but he was released about halfway through the season, and I had to stay there by myself. My first full year was in 1962, when I went to Boise, Idaho. That was in C ball. Then in 1963, I played AA ball in Austin, Texas, and had a good year there."

At the end of the season, Sandy came back to Guayama and married his hometown sweetheart. He was 20. Maria was 19. Shortly afterwards, they moved into a house in a brand new middle class neighbourhood called Monserrate in Salinas, a town a few miles to the west. The houses there are single-storey white stucco rectangles, some with pink or orange tile roofs, all of them with elaborate, white-painted iron grillwork across the front. The streets are narrow and the houses are tiny by North American standards, close together with no real yards. Among families and among neighbours, there is naturally a great degree of intimacy. Everyone knows everyone else, and knows them very well indeed. Children move from house to house, watched and fed and loved by a host of extra parents.

In the house in Salinas, Maria settled into life as a baseball wife. It was certainly not a traditional marriage, and more complicated in Puerto Rico at the time than it might be in the United States. In the early 1960s, minor league baseball players were paid a pittance, and few major leaguers fared that much better. They spent long stretches of time on the road and made do on meagre meal allowances. Bringing a wife along — especially a wife from a far-off island — was almost unheard of. The pattern that would hold for the next twenty years of the Alomars' life developed. In the spring, Sandy would leave for the mainland. In the summer, Maria would sometimes join him for a few weeks, as would the children. In the fall, he would finish the season, and then come home to rejoin the family and play winter baseball in the Puerto Rican league.

"It was tough," Sandy says. "Any ballplayer, if he's going to get married, has to have a special wife. It's not easy when you have to leave her behind. I married after the 1963 season, and then went back to the States in 1964. We started having babies in 1965, so she didn't go with me until 1967. I've seen a lot of players who get married and the wife is not supportive of her husband's career and that's wrong. That's why you see a lot of divorce around."

The 1964 season had been a breakthrough for Sandy. He started the year with the AAA Denver Bears, and then was called up to the big leagues by the Braves for September. It was a tribute not just to his ability, but to his attitude towards his chosen profession — an attitude that would later be adopted wholeheartedly by his sons.

By all accounts, Sandy Alomar wasn't a particularly gifted ballplayer. "He was no star," says former major league manager Jack McKeon, who would later hire Sandy as a coach with the San Diego Padres. "But he was a very smart player. He probably got the maximum out of his ability. He was a good-field no-hit guy in his early days, but worked at it and became a decent hitter. He had great baserunning instincts and he was a good base stealer, a good bunter. He made himself into one hell of a ballplayer when he didn't have as much talent as God might have given him."

He was also a Latino, which meant that he already had one strike against him in the conservative — as well as overtly and implicitly racist — baseball environment of the 1960s. "I felt like I had to keep my job," Sandy says. "That's what I wanted to do. People sometimes say that you're lazy — people who don't understand Latin people, who don't understand that we have a different way of doing things. It's just our natural way. So I was always there on time. I didn't miss games. I played when I was injured. I never asked for a rest. I worked when I had to work.

"My attitude was that if you're going to do something, you ought to do it well. If you're not going to do it well, what's the sense of staying there wasting your time? And Latins have to work harder. That's just common sense. They already have players over there in the United States. So they're not going to come to one of the islands just to get a guy with the same ability as the guy already over there. If you wanted to play, you couldn't have the same ability as that guy. You had to become better. I wanted to be better. I wanted to excel. I wasn't bigger than the other guys, so I had to take advantage of anything I could, any way I could cheat that would help me win the game. By cheat, I mean taking advantage of the little things, the little mistakes the other team makes.

"I was always watching people and talking to them. I asked players how they played their position, why they played like that. I asked the second baseman, the shortstop. I played with guys like Luis Aparicio, Jim Fregosi, Hank Aaron, Vada Pinson, Tommy Davis, Brooks Robinson. Those guys were superstars, and they had the right attitude for the game. Brooks Robinson wasn't a good runner and he didn't have a good arm, but he knew how to play the game and he played the game almost perfectly. That has to give you an incentive when you see a guy like that. You see yourself with a little bit of ability. Why would you waste it, when you can take advantage of it, plus take advantage of the mind you have?"

Sandy's hard work and dedication finally paid off when he made the Milwaukee Braves opening-day roster in 1965. "They converted me to a second baseman that year," he explains. "Denis Menke had hit twenty home runs the year before and he said that he didn't want to play second. I was a rookie, so I got to play second." He would hold a job in the major leagues for the next fourteen years and in the process play every position but pitcher and catcher.

That same year, the Alomars began their family. Sandia, a daughter, was born on July 4. The next year came Sandy Jr., and two years after that the baby of the family, Roberto.

"My Mom took care of me, my sister and my brother," Roberto says. "It was real tough for her. She was the kind of Mom who didn't want any help. She wanted to do everything herself. When you have to raise three children by yourself, it's not easy. My Dad worked hard to give us a good life. He didn't want Mom to work."

The three Alomar children were raised within what amounted to a large extended family of friends and relatives in Monserrate. Salinas was a safe, trusting place then, as it is to a somewhat lesser degree now. In those days the neighbourhood children could troop off together to the centre of town to watch a movie, with their parents secure in the knowledge that everyone they passed would know them and look out for them and tell their parents if anything went awry. The kids played in the streets, in a nearby vacant lot that served as a baseball diamond, and neighbours' houses were as welcoming and familiar as their own.

While the Alomar siblings were close in age and were close emotionally, they grew up with very different personalities. Sandia, who is shy and pretty, is regarded by the family as a mirror image of her mother. "Sandia was born on July 4 and her mother was born on July 10, so they have the same sign," Sandy Sr. says.

"My sister is really quiet," Roberto says. "We never had any problems with her. She's really intelligent — she got 4.0 grades all the time in school. She didn't play any sports — that's the weird thing. She just went to school. When she went to college, she used to be in her room all the time, studying, studying, studying.

She really wanted to make something of herself."

"Sandia wasn't really an athlete," Sandy Jr. says. "She's fragile. And she knew that she didn't have the advantage we had. We could play baseball. She knew that she had to work hard to get a scholarship. I think it was kind of hard for her, seeing two brothers playing major league baseball. She saw what kind of opportunities men have in life."

Sandy Jr. is a different package, a fun-loving, thrill-seeking extrovert. He is dark-skinned like his father, was always very tall and always seemed to be smiling. "Sandy was the kid who liked everything," his mother says. "He liked to go out with us, he liked to play outside, he liked to play with the neighbours. He liked everything dangerous. When he was little, he liked to put together little model airplanes. He had many of them filling his room. He told me he would go to school and become a pilot."

"Sandy likes to keep moving," his father says. "He likes dangerous stuff. He likes to talk to everybody. He's always laughing, always smiling at people. Robbie is more like me. Sandy is more independent. He likes to do things his own way. He is his own man."

"Sometimes, I think that Sandy hasn't grown up yet," says Carmen Pabon, who has lived across the street from the Alomars in Salinas for thirty years and who is Maria's closest friend. "He's still like a child — his expressions, the way he plays, the way he talks. He's got a child's face, like a baby face. And he's so big. I remember when he was a little boy, he was sitting in the street and playing with these little remote control cars. It was dark, so we could only see the lights on the cars going up and down. I said to my husband, 'I don't know if I'm seeing wrong, but I think I see something going up and down the street.' But I don't see anybody out there. Sandy was hiding behind a tree. He was making a joke on us. Then a little kid came up behind the car. He was going to grab it, and just as he reached for it, Sandy hit the button and the car went, whoosh, away. The little kid was so scared. And then Sandy started laughing."

"Sandy and I were always close," Roberto says. "We are still good friends. He was always more outgoing than me. When we lived in the States, he always made friends. He could speak English real well. He used to go outside and find some friends and I'd follow him. He did all the talking. When we were kids we had a few fights, but we weren't fighting all the time. I'd jump on him and he'd grab my hands. I have a scratch right here on my face. It's from when he pushed me and I hit the corner of the table and smashed my face. Eighteen stitches! You should have seen Sandy and Sandia — they were so scared. They were hiding under the table. When my mother asked 'Who did it?' they didn't say anything."

Being an Alomar male, Sandy Jr. of course played baseball, but from an early age he also developed other interests — model airplanes, karate and especially riding motorcycles and go-karts. "He was wild on the motorcycles," Roberto says. "I remember one time some policemen were following him and he lost them by riding through a river. He knew all the spots where they could not catch him. One time we went out on his motorcycle and he was driving, I was sitting behind. He was going up mountains, and then he jumped over a great big hole. I said, 'Hey, take me home.' And then one time in the go-kart, he smashed into a tree."

"I did some crazy stuff," Sandy Jr. says. "I think back and I wonder why the hell I was doing that stuff. It didn't make any sense, but when you're a kid you really don't think about that."

"It was hard for me because sometimes he would go out with the neighbours on the motorcycles and I would worry," says Maria. "He said, 'Don't worry, there is no danger for me, Mommy.' He would go to the mountains and come back very late. I told him I didn't want to see him over there because he could get killed. Sometimes, though, he said he wanted to play baseball. I asked him 'what position do you want to play?' and he said he wanted to be a catcher. 'I want my head working all the time,' he said. 'If my head is not working all the time, I don't feel comfortable.' "

And then there was Roberto, the quiet little boy with the big brown eyes and long, curly, almost-blonde hair that hung down to his shoulders. "Robbie was timid, quiet, scared," Sandy says. "When he was little he would never leave his mother." But his father was his idol because of the passion they shared.

"Roberto," says his mother, "was born in baseball."

"He was infatuated with it," Sandy Jr. says. "He was just nuts about the game."

Every story about Roberto Alomar's childhood seems to begin with a little boy and a ball and glove and a bat. "I remember when Robbie was a year and a half old," Carmen Pabon says. "He was still in diapers. No clothes, just the diaper. He used to get a baseball cap and put it on sideways, a big bat, a glove. He put the glove on his hand, carried the ball in his other hand, and tried to put the bat under his arm. He couldn't hold everything because he was so little. He crossed the street over to my house. He was so cute."

He would organize the games in the street or in a field. He would bring the equipment and he would have to bat first — or he and the equipment would go home. "Sandy used to get mad at him for that," his father remembers. Every Christmas Robbie asked Santa Claus for the same things — a new glove, a new bat, a new ball. Later he played a little basketball and enjoyed it, but really there weren't any other hobbies, there weren't any other interests — at least until girls caught his eye. Roberto was as single-minded as any child could be.

"He always wanted to play baseball when he was a little boy," Sandia says. "If we went some place, he had to have his bat and glove. Sandy liked motorcycles, Sandy liked airplanes, Sandy liked anything dangerous. Robbie was frightened of those things. He only liked baseball. He'd wake up in the morning and he'd want to play with his friends. When he played in the street, he always had to bat."

Roberto's all-encompassing love of baseball didn't leave room for much of anything else in his life, and that included school. The Alomars made education a priority for their children, sending them to private schools, setting them up with tutors when they spent summers in the United States, and encouraging them in their studies. "My mom and dad were always more concerned about school than sports because school is real important," Roberto says.

Sandia was the most committed student of the three, going on to graduate from university with an arts degree. Both Roberto and Sandy Jr. finished high school before pursuing their baseball careers full-time. But everyone in the family says that getting Robbie up in the morning, getting him to school and getting him through school was a struggle, especially for his sister and his mother. In the winter, he spent many weeknights at his father's games, often not returning home until well past midnight.

The next morning he didn't exactly leap out of bed inspired to learn.

"I always had to help Robbie with his school work," Sandia says. "Sandy did all his work, but Robbie's a little lazy. He didn't like school too much. He was a good student, but the problem with Robbie was that he never wanted to wake up early."

Maria took it upon herself to make sure Roberto never missed a class. "If he had a test, he would take his books to the ballpark, study at the ballpark," she says. "When his dad was playing in the winter league, sometimes we wouldn't get back from the games until 1:30 in the morning. I told him, if you want to go to the ballpark with your dad, you have to get up early. Sometimes in the morning, I had to put his socks on in bed. Sometimes I cleaned him in bed. He said, 'I'm tired, mom. I'm too tired.' At breakfast, I would even go over there and feed him.

"One time, his dad told him, 'You can't go to the ballpark, you have to stay home and study.' And he came up with a plan. He called me and he said 'Mom, I have a tape with my school work on it. When I go to sleep, you put on the tape, and then you put the tape recorder right beside my ear.' He went to sleep, I put on the tape, and the next day he had the test. It was perfect. It's incredible. It worked."

Despite the torture of having to get up in the morning, those were the best times in Roberto's childhood. It was fun in the winter, when his father was home and playing baseball nearly every night, when his family was together. And it was fun being the son of a local hero.

Being an Alomar carried with it plenty of cachet on

the island. In the big leagues, Sandy would always be a journeyman. He never earned a huge salary for the time — much less anything like the salaries of today — though combined with his winter league earnings it was enough for comfortable middle class existence for his family in Salinas. But whatever his status in the States, Sandy came home to Puerto Rico each fall a star.

"In the Puerto Rican league, he was a leader," says Jerry Morales, a winter league teammate who finished his major league career with the Chicago Cubs. "He was the kind of player who made things happen."

"He was one of the best second basemen I ever saw in the Puerto Rican league," says Jose Cruz, a former star with the Houston Astros. "He got over a thousand hits, he led the league almost every year in stolen bases, and one year in hitting. He played hard, because I don't think he had the chance to play regularly in the major leagues."

On the weekend, the whole Alomar family would go to the park in Ponce or San Juan and watch Sandy play. But during the week, just Robbie and Sandy Jr. — and many times, just Robbie — would make the trip with their father. Sandy Jr. was occasionally content to stay behind with his mother, sister, friends and motorcycles, but Robbie rushed home from school, knowing that he had to be back in Monserrate in time to catch his father before he left for the game.

"I had to run from school," Robbie says. "I had to get to our house real quickly so I could go with him."

"He was the guy that I couldn't leave behind," Sandy says. "If I couldn't take him to the game one day, I had to sneak out of the house. If he saw me go out the door without taking him to the ballpark, he would cry the whole night. I had to sneak away or I had to take him to almost every game.

"One time, I remember Robbie was supposed to stay at home while my Dad drove to San Juan to play a game," Sandy Jr. says. "That's about an hour away from our house. Well, Roberto hid behind the seat in the car. He didn't pop up until my Dad was about twenty miles away from the house and couldn't come back. That was funny as hell."

Anyone who was around Puerto Rican winter ball at the time remembers the Alomar boys, and especially remembers Roberto. They had the run of the ballpark, working out with the players before a game, shagging flies and fielding grounders, getting someone to pitch to them. Sometimes they would act as batboys during the game, other times they'd just hang out in the clubhouse or play their own game in an area behind the outfield fence. "A lot of times, Sandy would be in the clubhouse, looking for his glove," remembers Maco Oliveras, a winter league teammate. "He'd find the kids with it in the outfield.

"I remember since the first day I saw Robbie. You could tell that he had that talent," Oliveras continues. "Playing catch, running, hitting and the way he walked — he walked just like his dad. There was something about him that showed he had been around baseball, that he knew about baseball. There was something special about Robbie."

What he knew was what he learned from his father, the baseball gospel according to Sandy Alomar. "My Dad is a big influence on me," Roberto says. "I wanted to be like him. He's a real disciplined guy. Whenever you got out of line, he would tell you. We respect him. But we weren't intimidated by him. He was our father, but he treated us more like a friend. That's real important. He wasn't the kind of Dad who used to come and hit us all the time with his belt. Sometimes, though, he would have to tell us something, and we respected his decision."

Everything about Sandy Sr.'s major league career was a tribute to his work ethic, to his attitude, to his diligence and to his knowledge as much as to his talent. Through his experience, Sandy had developed some very strongly held opinions about the game he loved and the way it should be played. There was a right way and a wrong way for everything — not just about how you advanced a runner from first with nobody out, or how you positioned yourself to make the pivot in the double play, but how you ran onto the field to start an inning, how you ran out a hopeless groundball, how you acquitted yourself in the clubhouse and in front of the media. There were no shortcuts, there was no room for attitude, there was no showing up an opponent. If you were to succeed, you had to study the game, to understand its nuances. Even though his sons would be blessed with more natural ability than he ever had, they would learn to regard baseball as though their careers hung on every play.

"I tried to explain to them about the game, why things work the way they do, what they should do, why and how," Sandy Sr. says. "It's not just hitting, running, throwing and fielding. There are a lot of things involved in the game. You can win a game by anticipating the play. You might win a game by knowing how many outs there are. You might win a game by thinking, if this happens, we have to do it this way."

Luis Rosa, the leading professional scout in Puerto Rico and the man who would eventually sign both of the Alomar brothers for San Diego, remembers once talking to Sandy Sr. while Roberto was fielding grounders. "A ball took a bad hop and hit him in the mouth," Rosa says. "He came up to his father, and blood was pouring out of his mouth."

"I told him, if you want to be a player, you'd better stop crying," Sandy remembers. "I told him to put some ice in his mouth and get back out there. I was trying to teach him that he wasn't going to be treated any differently than anyone else, and that you have to learn from all the bad things."

During those winters spent with his father at the ballpark and on the drive back to Salinas, Roberto absorbed it all — the game, the way it's played, and especially the way his father felt it *should* be played. When you hear Roberto talk about baseball now, the words are Sandy's.

"You have to know how to play this game," Roberto says. "You have to be smart. It's not like you have to read books or anything like that, but you have to know what to do to be a better ballplayer. You have to understand the situations. Every day, you can learn something new — if you want to."

Today, baseball people marvel at Roberto Alomar's instinct for the game, his knack for being in the right position, for making the right decision, for being unselfish and understanding each situation. What they're really noticing are the results of some thorough lesson learned during the idyllic winters of his childhood.

Life wasn't quite so idyllic the rest of the year, though. At the end of February, Sandy would leave for spring training, and the family would be apart until school ended in June. Then Maria and the kids would fly to join him wherever he was playing in the United States — New York, Chicago, Anaheim, Dallas. "It was tough for me, because I was real close to my Dad,"

Roberto says. "I was the guy who always liked the game, and who always wanted to be like him. When he'd go to the States, I was disappointed because I wanted to see my Dad. I wanted to go to the games and I couldn't. I was really sad."

It was a tough time for everyone. "It was hard," Maria says. "I could have gone, but I wanted to keep my family together."

"I used to call," Sandy says. "I thought about them all the time. We would write each other every day."

Roberto remembers a particularly traumatic summer when the family was living in Texas. Sandy was on a road trip when the news came that his mother had died in Puerto Rico. "We couldn't go back to the funeral," he says. "My mom called my dad. He said you guys stay there, because it would have been expensive. We weren't rich. The most my Dad ever made playing baseball was forty or fifty thousand dollars. So we couldn't see her when she died, and she was a real good grandma."

But there were some good times as well. Going to an American city each summer was an adventure. "I loved the States," Sandia says. Predictably, Sandy Jr. was always the first to make himself at home in the new setting. He spoke the best English, and his personality transcended any situation. "Sandy Jr., the first day in a new city, he'd check everything out," Maria says. "He'd see a ballpark, and he'd want to go over there right away. Robbie is quiet. He's shy. But Sandy — no. He'd go over there and other kids would be practising and he'd say 'I'm Sandy Alomar Jr., I want to play.' And Robbie would follow after him."

The brothers would sometimes hang around the major league park where their father was playing, though the rules about what kids could and couldn't do were much more strict than in Puerto Rico. Sandy remembers that Robbie, when he was two years old, could identify all of his father's California Angels teammates by numbers. There is a picture in the Alomars' home of both boys sitting in a dugout with Hank Aaron. And Robbie remembers some of his more noteworthy playmates: "We used to play together with Barry Bonds, Ken Griffey Jr., and other kids."

"We played paper cup baseball in the hallways in the stadium," Sandy Jr. remembers. "Me and Roberto and Barry Bonds and Barry's brother Rickey. You get a Coca Cola cup and crunch it up to make a ball out of it and hit it with your hand. We played two against two."

When it was time for school to begin, the children and their mother would head back to Puerto Rico to await Sandy's return at the end of the season. Back home, while his father was away playing ball, Roberto formed one of the most important relationships in his life. Nestor Pabon, Carmen Pabon's brother-in-law, lived in the neighbourhood and ran a pharmacy in Salinas' small business district. He hired Robbie to work there after school, and soon would become almost a surrogate father.

"I called him my second dad," Roberto says. "When I was young, I worked for him in the pharmacy. He used to give me twenty-five dollars a week. He lived three houses from our house. He had three daughters, but he didn't have any boys, and so I was like his boy. He had a beach house, where we used to go swimming with his daughters. And he had a speed boat that we used to go out on and drive around.

"There's not that many people that I trust. He was one of them. He was a great person, the kind of person that helped me whenever my Dad wasn't there. I didn't get into trouble because he took care of me. He told me, 'Roberto, you have to stay away from the bad things.' He taught me how to be a good human being."

3

◇ THE FAMILY BUSINESS

There are nearly two thousand pages in the *Baseball Encyclopedia*, detailing the minutiae of the history of the professional big leagues. Flipping through them you come to understand the odds. Every player to ever suit up in a game of major league baseball, even for a single inning or a single at-bat, is listed: his name, his birthdate, his height, his weight, his nickname. From these pages W.P. Kinsella plucked one of those one-at-bat wonders, Archibald "Moonlight" Graham, and made him a star.

Many careers can be summed up in a single line of type. A lot more can be summed up in a very short paragraph. Five years in the game is exceptional, ten years is extraordinary, a career longer than that — even in baseball's current, watered-down form, where free agency makes hanging on past your prime more worthwhile than ever — is usually the mark of someone special.

Sandy Alomar, who played fifteen years in the big

leagues, was a special ballplayer, but not for the usual reasons. His major accomplishments can't be measured statistically. There's no way of quantifying what it means to be a reasonably talented infielder from a little town in Puerto Rico, to sign a contract and head to a foreign land where there are plenty of players with far greater raw abilities than your own. Then, through brains and guts and hard work, you find your niche. When the niche is gone, you find another team. Fifteen years and six teams later you retire, essentially on your own terms.

Sandy Alomar knew enough not to relax after he landed a spot on the Milwaukee Braves roster in 1965. He understood that he didn't have the luxury of becoming a prima donna, of being able to count on a starting job, or even to count on a position as his own. He was a journeyman professional, pure and simple, a worker who never took his job for granted.

"Sandy was a good organization man. He did what the organization asked of him," says Luis Rosa, a long-time friend and the premier major league scout in Puerto Rico. "He knew his limitations. He was very versatile. He could play many positions, and I think that was one of the things that kept him in the game for such a long time."

"I felt like if you don't fit with one team and there's another one interested in you, you go," Sandy says. "As long as you have a big league name on your shirt, that's all that really matters. You know that somehow, somewhere, you're doing something right. The teams are looking for something that they need, a piece of the puzzle. One of the things that I did was that I always tried to play in different positions, because that is valuable for a team. By doing that and doing whatever I was told — I very seldom complained, I very seldom said anything — I think that extended my career."

The most money Sandy earned during his decade and a half in the majors was perhaps $50,000, a far cry from what today's players — including his sons — can haul in for a 162-game season. But his salary was never really the issue.

"When Sandy played, there was no money," Maria says. "Baseball is different now. Now it's a business. Money wasn't important in our life because money doesn't make people really happy. When Sandy was playing, he would have played for nothing."

In December 1966, the Braves traded Sandy, Eddie Matthews and Arnie Umbach to Houston in exchange for Dave Nicholson and Bob Bruce. He never played a regular-season game for the Astros — instead he was traded during the final week of spring training to the New York Mets for Derrell Griffith. In August, he moved on to his fourth team in nine months, going to the Chicago White Sox in a straight cash deal.

Sandy stayed in Chicago until May, 1969, when he and Bob Priddy were traded to the California Angels for Bobby Knoop. "A trade is always for the best," he says. "If they don't want you in one place, go to the other one." The move to Anaheim, though, was particularly fortuitous. Sandy's manager with the Angels was Harold (Lefty) Phillips. For the first time in a long time Sandy would be treated like something other than a utility player. Phillips gave Sandy a chance to start every day.

"I really have to appreciate what he did for me," Sandy says. "Lefty Phillips believed in me all the time. He let me play — I had a streak of 648 consecutive games in California."

Since the Angels weren't winning any championships, that ideal situation couldn't possibly last. The team went from ten games over .500 in 1970 to ten games under .500 in 1971, and Phillips was fired. Del Rice took over the team in 1972, and then Bobby Winkel moved into the manager's office in 1973. He decided to put an end to Sandy's streak because he felt the pressure of keeping it going was affecting his play. "That was very sad because I was giving my best all the time," Sandy says. "I was in a slump, but every player goes through slumps. That's part of the game."

Statistically, the 1971 season had been Sandy's best in the majors. He led the league with 689 at-bats, hit .260 and drove in 42 runs. But it was the season before that provided one of his biggest thrills — an invitation to play in the All Star Game. "That's the highlight for every player," he says. "As an individual, it's the All Star Game, and as a team it's the World Series."

The Series would have to wait awhile. In 1974, Dick Williams took over as manager of the Angels, and Sandy saw his playing time drastically reduced. For the first time in his career, the "organization man" decided it was time to speak out for himself. "I wasn't playing, and I thought I was still young enough to play," he remembers. "So I went to the manager and asked to be traded. I didn't go to the press or anything like that. I just went straight to the people that I had to."

His wish was granted and he was sent to the New York Yankees in another cash deal. For Sandy, the Yankees represented a great opportunity, his first real crack at winning a championship. Much of the talent was already there and other players were added during Sandy's first year: Chris Chambliss and Graig Nettles, Thurman Munson and Sparky Lyle, Willie Randolph and Mickey Rivers, Jim (Catfish) Hunter and Lou Piniella. Finally, halfway through the 1975 season, the last piece of the puzzle was put in place when the fiery Billy Martin took over as manager, his first stint with his beloved Yankees.

"It was great," Sandy says. "In 1975, when Billy came over to the Yankees, I remember Ed Brinkman, who had played for Martin in Detroit, telling me that he wished he could be there because Billy was going to make a winner out of this club. He did, and it was a lot of fun. The only thing Billy Martin asked of his players was to give one hundred percent. He didn't care what you did outside the game. The only thing he cared about was what you did at the ballpark, how you played the game — and he didn't like any excuses. If you messed it up, you messed it up. Just admit it to him, and he would leave you alone. He didn't like to have a lot of young players around because of the way he was — he was always yelling and he was always saying things that a minute later he wouldn't even remember. The young players would carry that with them. He was worried that the younger players would hold grudges and that they'd feel uncomfortable with him, then get nervous and make mistakes. But the older players wouldn't care what he said. They understood Billy."

"It was a great team, a team that was always close. Most of the winning teams are like that. If you went out to have a drink after a game, you'd have six or seven or eight guys together. It was never just two here and two there."

Maria wasn't crazy about moving her children to Queens for the summer — "The cars, they just go every-where," she remembers, rolling her eyes — but for the kids it was just another adventure. "I started scouting in New York," Rosa says. "I used to go to see the Yankees when they were playing in Shea Stadium because Yankee Stadium was being renovated. I can remember sitting with these two little kids. Sandy Jr. and Robbie were sitting there eating ice-ream while I was freezing to death."

The Yankees won the American League East by a comfortable ten-and-a-half-game margin in 1976, and then went on to face the Kansas City Royals — an expansion team that had reached its first playoff — in the American League Championship Series. Sandy was limited to one, fruitless, at-bat during the series, though he was standing in the on-deck circle when Chris Chambliss hit the pennant-winning home run in the bottom of the ninth of game five.

So it was on to the World Series, where the Yankees would lose in four straight to Cincinnati's Big Red Machine, and Sandy would never get to the plate. Still, those games have an important place in the family's memories.

"I remember watching it on television," Roberto says. "It was great for my Dad, and for us too. But I didn't really know what it was all about. What's the big deal about the World Series? Now I can tell you what the big deal is. It's what you work for, it's why you go through all those painful moments."

The Yankees would win the Series the next season, and again in 1978, but Sandy wasn't around to share in the glory. In February 1977, he was traded to the Texas Rangers in return for Brian Doyle, Greg Pryor and cash. Arlington would turn out to be the final stop in his major league career. He played very little over two seasons in Texas, appearing in 69 games in 1977 and in only 24 — with just 29 at-bats — in 1978. He was a free agent at season's end, facing both a personal and professional crossroads.

"I was 34 years old, which now is considered still young for the game," Sandy remembers. "Maria asked me to retire. My contract had expired with Texas. They offered me the travelling instructor's job in their minor league system. Some other teams wanted me to go to spring training and try out. But Maria said, 'The kids are getting older. They're getting tougher to deal with when you're away. Why don't you stay home?' So I did."

Understandably, it was a traumatic decision for the family. Sandy and Maria had lived their entire married life around the baseball season. The children had never known anything else. Now, he would return home, where he would continue to play winter ball for another three years, but where it was also time to get on with a new life no longer centred on the game he loved.

"I was always prepared," Sandy says. "I wasn't the type of guy who was living way up here, and then just dropped out. I was always down to earth. I was always thinking ahead. I wasn't a big salary man. We had saved a little bit of money. After baseball we had to adjust. You go through the ups and downs in life. But I never needed to have much stuff around me. My wife always complained because I never bought a brand new car. I used to buy a used car, fix it up, use it while I was in Puerto Rico and then sell it when I went to the States.

"We always lived just like we live now. I never tried to live a fancy life. I don't believe in that. I believe in raising my kids, teaching them the right way, and staying with the type of people we should deal with. Why should I be a fake?"

Sandy gradually adjusted to being home, Maria adjusted to having him home, Sandy Jr. and Sandia got used to seeing their father around the house more often. But Roberto took Sandy's retirement very, very hard. His father the baseball player was his idol, and being around the game meant everything to him. Now, that part of his life was ending, and he wouldn't let it go without a fight.

"Robbie cried and begged me not to retire," Sandy says.

"Robbie was ten when Sandy quit," Maria says. "He cried. 'I want you back. I want Daddy to play baseball.' "

"We missed the game when he retired," Roberto says now. "We missed our life. But in another sense, we spent more time with our Dad, and that was really important, because sometimes you need the love of the family."

Sandy took some of his savings and bought a gas station in Salinas, a business that he decided would be his post-baseball career. Though he'd never earned an enormous salary as a baseball player, the new job was an economic comedown — less salary and more headaches. The Alomars' financial circumstances changed for the worse. Roberto remembers it as a difficult time for the family. "It was tough," he says. "Even though they didn't really tell us about it, I knew those were rough times. My Dad went through some bad times with investments. When you have money, everybody comes up to you and says, 'Hey, can you lend me money for this?' and then they never pay you back. My father has a big heart. He's too soft. They took his money, and whenever he had problems, he didn't have anybody to help him. He went to the bank and solved his problems himself. He learned the hard way and now he's teaching me that way. He doesn't want the same thing happening to us. People have already asked me for money, and I will not give it to them. I came a long,

long way. People think it started when I was 20. It started when I was six years old. If I didn't make it, nobody would have known me."

In fact, when Roberto was six years old, many people — baseball people — already knew him, just as they knew his brother. The Alomar boys had grown up in the game and in public. They didn't have to be discovered because from the time they were toddlers they were putting their baseball skills on display during the winters in Puerto Rico and during the summers at the major league ball-parks where their father played in the United States. They were regarded much like musical child prodigies: the talent was there, the instincts were there. The only question was how they would develop, whether they would retain the desire to play baseball through their teens, whether their adult bodies would be able to do what came so naturally when they were pre-adolescents.

Roberto's passion for the game was never really a question. His family, his friends, everyone knew that the only thing Robbie had ever wanted to be was a baseball player. And because he wasn't just playing, because even as a child he was studying and practising and perfecting, his physical talents only grew as he got older, along with his knowledge of the game.

"To Roberto, the ballpark was it," Luis Rosa says. "That was his university, that was his college. That was everything in his life — being out there, enjoying the fans, enjoying the people around him. He loved the other ballplayers and being around them. He knew he could make a nice life in baseball, and he's done that."

Sandy Jr. was a very different story: the son who, for a time anyway, rebelled and tried to chart a path independent of the family business. "He is his own man," his father says. "He likes to do things his way."

Or, as Sandy Jr. explains it himself: "It's like, if you had a father who worked in an ice-cream place, you'd get bored eating ice-cream every day."

Sandy Jr. obviously had the family's baseball gift, but as a boy he just wasn't as interested — or as much of a natural — as his younger brother. He was tall and skinny, and became a catcher not only because the position satisfied his need to be part of every play, but because he knew he didn't have quite the same physical assets as his baby brother.

"I didn't have the quickness Roberto had," he says. "I didn't have the great hands as an infielder. I could play the outfield, but I wasn't as fast as Robbie. I was bigger. Catching was a position where I thought I could be more aggressive, and where I was going to be in the game. I thought it was more interesting than any other position. And my Dad thought that it was the only position that would get me to the big leagues quickly. Otherwise, I would probably be struggling somewhere in the minor leagues right now."

At least as an adolescent, getting to the big leagues wasn't one of Sandy Jr.'s higher priorities. He was doing other things, thinking about other things, and eventually, he drifted away from the game altogether.

"I liked computers and I liked airplanes," he says. "I really enjoyed math. I was doing plenty of other stuff. I was even delivering papers. I couldn't tell you what I planned to do for a living, but it wasn't going to be baseball.

"I had the dirt bikes, and I took Tae Kwan Do for six or seven years. I really enjoyed that. It gave me a lot of peace of mind when I was young. You can really get rid of a lot of stress doing something like that.

"So when I was thirteen or fourteen years old, I just

stopped playing baseball. I was doing my own thing. My Dad didn't put any pressure on me. He left it up to me. He didn't stick his nose in. He just said, you have a natural talent and you're wasting it. But he didn't say much."

"I was concerned about the motorcycles," Sandy Sr. says. "I've always been scared of that. You know how kids are. They don't measure danger. One time, Sandy was riding in shorts, and there's an exhaust pipe on the bike. He burned his knee up, and that's when he started thinking about it a little bit. I told him if you want to do this motorcycle thing, you have to work hard, because there's not much money in this. At least in baseball, you have a better chance, and you know you have the ability. But the game just wasn't as important for Sandy as it was for Robbie."

Baseball would only become important for Sandy Jr. after it again became fun. The opportunity to re-enter the game came about by chance. "This guy came into my Dad's gas station, where I was hanging around, and asked me if I wanted to play in a small tournament. He needed a catcher for his team. I agreed to play, but only for a couple of games. Then I played a couple of games, and I played a couple of good games. A scout for an American Legion team was there. He saw me and asked me if I'd like to play for his team as a starting catcher. I didn't know what to say. I didn't want to commit myself and then not finish the season. So I thought about it and finally decided that yeah, I'm going to play. I had a good year in the American Legion league, and then another year, and I had fun. A lot of scouts saw me and thought I was a natural catcher, good hands, good arm, and that eventually my hitting would come around."

One of the scouts who saw Sandy Jr., as well as Robbie,

was Luis Rosa, who happened to be both a family friend and a very influential presence in Latin American baseball.

Rosa has made a career out of finding and nurturing the best baseball talent on the island. Though he is Puerto Rican, he had spent most of his life elsewhere, growing up as an Army brat and following his father around the world before finally settling with his family in New York City when he was fifteen years old. He played baseball, but never well enough to play professionally. When he first started some part-time scouting — or "bird dogging" — in New York for the Montreal Expos, he was making his living as an assistant bank manager. Bobby Ramos, who would make it to the big leagues, was the first player he signed.

Rosa's other pet project was the Raiders Youth Development Program, based in the Brownsville section of Brooklyn, the home neighbourhood of heavyweight boxing champions Mike Tyson and Riddick Bowe. His athletic programs, including baseball, were geared to helping the many Puerto Rican emigres living in what is one of the most depressed, drug-infested and dangerous ghettos in the United States.

In 1976, Rosa moved to Puerto Rico, where he would scout for the Expos, and where he would transplant his Raiders program. "I got off the plane and the next day I was organizing the team," he says. "The places were different but the needs were the same." Unlike the Dominican Republic, where baseball has become the single dream of so many otherwise hopeless young men, in Puerto Rico he found the game was no longer a national obsession.

"Baseball has always been the main sport here in the minds of many people because there was a Clemente, there was a Cepeda. There was a golden age of baseball in Puerto Rico. It's very much a part of the culture. But in the Dominican, it is a ticket to ride. It is a way out of poverty. Here we are more Americanized, we are in the same rhythm as the United States. A lot of people say that you don't find the real good strong baseball players here anymore."

Rosa took it upon himself to find them and to develop them — he has worked for six major league organizations, and is currently employed by the San Francisco Giants. Since 1988, he has operated a baseball academy at the Ciudad Deportiva Roberto Clemente complex in suburban San Juan, which is funded by the foundation run by Clemente's widow. Kids enter the program at age three and can stay until they're eighteen. Some of the more famous alumni of Rosa's teams include Benito Santiago, Edwin Correa, Juan Nieves, Ivan Calderon, Ivan Rodriguez, Luis Quinones and Mario Diaz. Santiago, Calderon and Rodriguez are among the thirty-three players Rosa has signed who have gone to the big leagues, along with Ozzie Guillen, Juan Gonzalez, Edwin Nunez and Orlando Mercado.

At the time the Alomar brothers were coming of age, Rosa just happened to be working for the San Diego Padres organization.

"I think from the age of thirteen or fourteen, I'd already started seriously looking at them," he says. "You always saw Roberto as having a little extra over Sandy. Roberto was more loosey-goosey. He knew that he had ability, he developed it, he enjoyed it. He played with the ball. The ball didn't play with him. He had a lot of inborn reflexes. Sandy had to work for what he got because for Sandy, baseball was something that he took up. It wasn't in him. He took it up and he developed it."

Rosa didn't have to go far to convince his boss that the Alomar boys were worth pursuing. Jack McKeon, the Padres' general manager at the time, had managed the Santurce Cangrejeros in the Puerto Rican winter league in 1976. One of his players was Sandy Alomar Sr., and so he saw what everyone else had seen.

"I remember watching those kids running around on the field and getting their father to pitch to them," McKeon says. "I could see that they were handling themselves pretty well even then. And they weren't rowdies, they weren't getting in your way, and they had a pretty good idea of how to play this game, all at seven or eight years old. I can relate to that, because I had two boys, and when I travelled and managed in the big leagues my kids were the same way. They were exposed to major league players all the time. They picked up all the lingo, the terminology, the know how and the mannerisms. That made them a little more advanced than the other kids."

As the eldest, Sandy was the first of the Alomar brothers to be eligible to sign a major league contract when he was seventeen years old. He was scouted and there was strong interest, but it took awhile before a serious offer arrived. "There were a few guys looking at him," Sandy Sr. says, "but it was nothing like it would be with Robbie."

"Sandy was not a really highly coveted prospect down there," says San Diego *Times Union* baseball writer Barry Bloom. "Robbie was."

"Before I decided on signing Sandy, it took me three tryouts over a year," Rosa remembers. "I went out there and every time he improved a little bit. He started getting interested in the game. He was into karate and other sports, but one of the things I enjoyed was watching his interest in baseball develop. The third tryout, he threw a couple to third base, a couple to second base. He swung the bat and then I said, 'Let's go, you're ready to go,' and I signed him."

Sandy signed with the Padres in 1984, and was assigned to Spokane of the Northwest League, a rookie league. His departure, alone, for the United States, was an emotional moment for the family. "He was going to Washington, a long way away," Maria says. "I cried. Everybody cried. I wanted him to go over there and play hard for the family. But I was crying because he would be so far away."

Next it would be Robbie's turn, and there was no question how the Padres hierarchy — and every scout on this island — felt about his potential. This one was a no-brainer.

"Roberto, the minute I saw him, I wanted to sign him. I was going all out for him," Rosa says. "Even as a teenager, he was a complete ballplayer. He could run, hit, throw. He occasionally would hit with power. He had great fielding hands. He had all the top qualities, so what else were you looking for? And he grew up in the game. There are some guys who are born to the game, who *are* the game, who don't just play the game."

"First of all, you looked at his size," McKeon says. "You saw that he had an agile body. There was quickness, there was the same quickness you saw when he was a seven-year-old kid, or a nine-year-old kid or a fourteen-year-old kid. He could run. But the biggest things were his baseball instincts and how he reacts. If you watched him play in a game, you'd think *hey, this guy's got something there.*"

As he had with Sandy Jr., Sandy Sr. acted as his son's advisor. Because the boys were minors, he would have to give final approval to any contract they signed. He says, "The team knew that before they could do anything, the boys had to come to me. So all I did was take them to some tryouts in San Juan and watch. I had to sign the contracts anyway. Before the boys signed, if they didn't understand the contract, or they didn't understand what people were telling them, they could get the information from people who knew."

The Padres had the inside track from the beginning, because of both Rosa's and McKeon's relationship with the family, and because they had already signed Sandy Jr. They also had something else up their sleeve.

Since he had left baseball, Sandy Sr. had grown restless in the gas station business and hoped that somehow he might be able to return to the game. "I wanted to go back into the game because the boys were going to be playing," he remembers. "They were grown up, and what we had wanted to do in Puerto Rico was raise them. The thing that I had done all my life was baseball, and I just wanted to go back because I felt like I had a lot of knowledge that I could give."

But — as is the case with most Latin American veterans — there weren't a wealth of opportunities or offers. While blacks slowly have managed to make inroads in the coaching and managerial ranks of the major leagues, Latins have been largely shut out. "They didn't have that real solid education to become managers and coaches," Rosa says. "It was limited. There was a language barrier, there was racism, there were many things in baseball. They were like the third party in the game. First you had the whites, then you had the blacks, and then you had the Latins. I have always said the

Puerto Ricans did not get ready for life after the game. Because of their lack of knowledge of the language, they didn't fit in, and they didn't develop to the level that you would want them to."

At the same time, the smart teams were placing more and more emphasis on recruiting and developing Latin American ballplayers. The Padres, who were then moving in that direction, and who had a number of fine Latin American prospects in their system, decided they needed a Spanish-speaking minor league instructor. "I find myself very, very responsible for getting Sandy back into the game," Rosa says. "He had the gas station down in Salinas. I remember telling him, 'Sandy, you are wasting a lot of the knowledge you had of baseball. This is not where you belong. You belong in baseball.' When I signed his first son, I told Jack McKeon, Jack, why don't we hire Sandy Alomar Sr.? I think that he could definitely be an asset to this program. We are going to get very heavily involved in Latin America. I think he could be a very good strong help to us."

It didn't hurt that Sandy already had one son in the system, and had another that San Diego desperately wanted to sign.

"I knew he wanted to get back in baseball," McKeon says, "so I told him I'd give him a job. That was the first time I was in a general manager's position where I could go around and tell someone, I'll take care of you. He said he'd be interested just as soon as he could get rid of the service station. I figured it this way — if I got two of them, I was going to get the third one. I figured I've got the catcher and I've got the old man, now I'm going to get the third one. The mother, Maria, wanted all three of them together, and so I had the in."

The Padres came to Sandy Sr. with their offer for

Robbie, and he and his son accepted the deal. "I gave my word to the Padres, and that was the bottom line," Sandy says. "The organization was a good bet for both Robbie and Sandy Jr. A lot of time you might get a $100,000 bonus, but that doesn't mean it will bring you to the big leagues. But if you get $50,000 and the club guarantees you that you're going to get to the big leagues in a certain amount of time, you have to look into that too. Sandy had Benito Santiago in front of him, but the way I look at it, there's always some other team. You never know what's going to happen — Benny goes to the big leagues, Sandy is in AAA and he's ready, and a lot of teams are after him. And Robbie was fortunate. He got to the Padres when they didn't have any infielders. All they had to do was play well through the minor leagues."

There was a last-minute complication. Other than San Diego, Roberto's most persistent suitor had been the Toronto Blue Jays. That year, the expansion franchise was about to come into its own, winning the American League's Eastern Division title for the first time and coming within a win of a spot in the World Series. The team's front office — and particularly executive vice president Pat Gillick — had developed a reputation as one of the most shrewd in baseball, plucking talent from other organizations, trading wisely, signing fine prospects. Latin Americans had been a major portion of the team's early success, with stars like George Bell, Damaso Garcia, Alfredo Griffin and later Tony Fernandez. Gillick knew Sandy Sr. from the days when both were employed by the New York Yankees.

"Epy Guerrero [the team's Latin American co-ordinator] had seen him," Gillick says. "Then Al LaMacchia and Bob Mattick [the team's vice presidents of baseball] went to see him. They were really excited about him. But he knew that Luis Rosa was on him and that he was working for San Diego, so we thought it might be a done deal."

"Epy sent a guy to Puerto Rico, and he said something rude to my mom," Roberto remembers. "From that point on, we didn't pay any attention to him. After that, Epy fired him and there was a big scene. And then I almost signed with Toronto. Toronto was my second choice. But they had Damaso Garcia in Toronto at that time playing second. San Diego didn't have anybody. You don't want to stay in the minor leagues forever."

After Sandy had promised Roberto to Rosa and McKeon, Gillick took his shot, coming up with substantially more money than San Diego was willing to pay. "The offer that the Jays made was outstanding," Sandy says. "At the moment, I wasn't sure. Then Luis talked to me again and the Blue Jays talked to me again. But my word to me means more than a lot of money. So I just told Pat that I had already given my word."

In the spring of 1985, the Alomars left, as a family, for Charleston, South Carolina, home of the Padres A level farm team. Sandy Jr. would catch. Sandy Sr. would coach. Seventeen-year-old Roberto would play second base. Maria would cook and keep house and look after her family. It was a triumphant, happy time for everyone, but Maria may have enjoyed it the most.

"I wanted Robbie to play with his brother," she says. "I wanted him to stay with the family. Robbie had the chance to sign for more money. But the family was most important for me. My family, I wanted to keep close. That's the best thing that you can hope for your family."

4

◇ LEARNING THE ROPES

There were no tears in the spring of 1985 when the Alomars prepared to leave for the United States. After all of those years, all of those separations, this would be a special time for Maria, her husband, and her sons.

The men would go together to Yuma, Arizona, for spring training at the San Diego Padres minor league complex — Sandy Sr. back in the game he loved; Sandy Jr. already established in the minor leagues; Roberto a high-school graduate leaving home for the first time. Then they would report to Charleston, South Carolina, home of the Padres A level farm club, the Rainbows of the South Atlantic League, where each would have a job: coach, catcher and second baseman. They would live in the same house, and in the summer Maria would join them. They would be a family, together, and together again in baseball. Nothing could have made them happier.

"We lived together," Maria says. "That was wonderful. I could go to the ballpark early to watch my kids all the time. I went to see the workouts, and we talked about baseball. I could cook for them — they like my rice and beans. And I could watch out for Robbie. It is like I have antennae, I know when something is bothering him. I talked to him about baseball. I said it's a life where you never know what's going to happen. He said, 'Ma, I want this. I worked for this.'

"Robbie is confident in God. He says that God is the first one with me because He goes with me everywhere. I never pushed Roberto. I wanted him to go to university. But he told me that baseball was the best thing in his life. He said there are things he wants to prove. He said that if something happens and it doesn't work out, he will apply for college. 'You're never too old for college,' he said. 'I'm young and I don't want to lose this time. This time is most important in baseball.' "

"One of the things that really helped the boys was me being with them in 1985, when we were all together," Sandy Sr. says. "It is a big adjustment. But that year, they lived with us. Their mother was there cooking for them every day. It was just like being at home."

"It was a good year," Roberto says. "My dad taught me a lot of things. Sandy and I played in the All Star Game. Charleston was a great city to play baseball in. It helped me having my family there because I was the youngest one in the family. If I had been by myself, I would have been lost. It's good to have good advice, and what better advisor could you have than your dad?"

The ballpark must have seemed like home as well, since Roberto made an easy transition to being a professional. Even though he was only seventeen years old, he had no trouble with the new level of competition. He ended the year hitting .293 with 36 bases, had played in the league's All Star Game and had been voted by *Baseball America* — the most prestigious publication covering minor league ball — as the best young second base prospect in baseball. Meanwhile, Sandy Jr. refined his catching skills, though, as had been the case in the past, he struggled at the plate.

There were still some difficult personal adjustments to be made. Roberto and Sandy had never been coached by their father before. When they had played Little League, Sandy Sr. was off playing in the majors. Their mother actually had more to do with that part of their lives, often ferrying whole teams around in her station wagon when other transportation became scarce. Sandy had always been their baseball mentor, of course, but now for the first time he was also their boss.

Coaches have a special role on a baseball team. While a manager usually maintains a professional distance between himself and his players, a coach can be more intimate. Especially in the minor leagues, coaches are instructors, handling the day-to-day business of teaching players the game. They are also confidantes, comrades, buddies and intermediaries between the guys on the field and the guy at the top.

All of which gets complicated if one of your coaches is also your dad. "It was good for us," Roberto says. "All three of us were on the same team. We tried to look good for him. He's still your dad, but sometimes you can't look at it that way. You have to do your job."

Sandy Sr. had anticipated the situation when he accepted the job with the Padres. Since it was his first year back in baseball, and since he dearly wanted to stay, he had as much on the line as his sons. So he established a set of ground rules, ways of preserving the family relationships without letting them spill over into the workplace. It would come in handy a few years later, when father and son were again together in the major leagues.

"That's something we had talked about," Sandy Sr. says. "We separated one thing from the other. They know that when I'm on the field, they have to say my father is my coach — he's not my dad, and I'm not going to treat him like my dad. And I'm not going to treat them as my sons, despite the fact that we call each other father and son. We're separate. I'm a coach, they're players. Outside of the park, then we're father and sons again.

"Still, it caused a bit of jealousy from the other players because they thought I was going to show a bit of a preference for my kids. Sometimes, you actually have to be a little bit tougher on your own kids, and that's what's bad about it. People think that you're going to be extra nice to your kids, and you just try to change their minds by being a little bit harsh. But we had a good understanding, the boys and I."

The other thing Roberto had to become accustomed to was living and working in a foreign culture. Although he had spent all of those childhood summers in the United States — and despite the fact that his family was with him the first year — Roberto still needed time to begin to feel at home. By virtue of Puerto Rico's quasi-colonial status, he was born and remains a U.S. citizen. But also he comes from a place apart. He didn't feel at home in the United States, especially in those early years, and — like other Latin American players — he was treated as an outsider within the sport.

Twenty years before, his father had had to fight the prejudice that came with being a Latin American in the game, something he did by working hard, keeping quiet, and doing what the organization told him to do.

The early 1980s were different from the early 1960s. Legal segregation had been eliminated in the United States, schools had been integrated, baseball had its first black manager. But for Latin players, the changes had not been so dramatic. Many of the old stereotypes about players from the Caribbean persisted. In many ways, Roberto was treated just as his father had been treated.

"I know how it was in the old days," he says. "There was a lot of prejudice, a lot of racism. And there still is some of that. A lot of people assume that Latins are hard-headed. But not everybody is the same. We are good players. We know how to play the game. You have to realize that we come from another world. We leave our countries to go to the big world. Maybe it was less difficult for me because I'd been to the States. But I know people from the Dominican, they sign for a thousand-dollar bonus, and they don't know how to speak English, they don't know anything about the country. When you don't know much English and you don't have a lot of education, sometimes you say things that you don't mean to say. The media turns it around and puts it in a bad way, and people think that's the way Latins are.

"Just try putting yourself in the situation they're coming from. They come from really poor, poor places. They don't have any money. They come here with just a little education and they play the game — and then people say bad things about them. People say that they don't know how to speak the language, that they don't know how to react, that they have hot tempers. Then we have to play against Americans, because we're going to their world. We want to take their positions. That's why they're jealous of us. That's why we have to work double. We have to earn our position. When I went to the States, I had no friends. I just went there to do my job and let my ability do the talking."

His ability spoke volumes right from the beginning. A successful season in Charleston was followed by a fine year in Reno of the Class A California League in 1987, where he won the league batting title with a .346 average and made the All Star team, despite a series of nagging injuries, including a split lip and groin pull. "I saw him in Reno," Pat Gillick says. "I felt at the time that he had tremendous ability. I remember saying to someone, I wish we'd got the kid. He looks like he's going to be a player."

In the winter, he went home to live with his family and play in the Puerto Rican winter league against major leaguers, and more than held his own. "I saw him play for Caguas in the winter league in 1987," San Diego baseball writer Barry Bloom remembers. "I couldn't believe how poised he was compared to all the major leaguers who were down there just going through the motions. I looked at him and thought 'this kid's going to be a terrific major league player.' It took one game to see that. Defensively, especially playing on those terrible fields down there, he just had the grace and the movement and the range and the arm. You could see that right away."

Deacon Jones, a long-time baseball man, was coaching for the San Diego organization in 1987, when he first encountered Roberto. "I was in Yuma in the spring training with the Padres," he remembers. "His father and I coached together. Knowing Sandy — the type of guy he is, a great baseball man — and knowing that his kids had been in the game all their lives, I expected they would be like him, hardworking and intelligent. I saw the same work ethic in Robbie. The thing that impressed me the most was I remember one night we were playing an exhibition game on one of the diamonds at our home park in Arizona. We had our hitting tunnels on the same diamond, down along the side of the field. I remember the game starting, and at that point the minor leaguers were supposed to be through for the day. Robbie was down in the cage hitting and bunting when the game started. In about the seventh or eight inning, I looked up and he was still down there. I said to Sandy, 'Look at your kid down there. He's still down there working on his bunting and hitting and everything.' Sandy turned to me and said, 'He was trained that way.' I thought that was very impressive. That gives you some idea about the boy. He works to excel. He had the ability, but he enhanced it through his work ethic. That's special.

"Later I watched him play, and it was like watching Sandy — he tries to find a way to beat you. He was brought up that way. It's really a reflection on his dad. Roberto has tremendous instincts. You don't see many guys coming up with that many tools. You find a ballplayer now, coming up to the big leagues, he'll have one or two tools. A DH is a guy with just one tool. Robbie had it all — glove, bat, legs, arm. That's very unusual, and that's why he's a star."

"One of the things I always taught my kids was to prepare yourselves in the minor leagues, because when you finally get to the big leagues, you don't want to get sent down," Sandy Sr. says. "Getting sent down is the worst thing that ever happens to a player. It's just like going from heaven to hell. I try to tell the young kids, prepare yourselves for when you go up, otherwise you're only going to be there for a cup of coffee. And that cup of coffee will taste better than a steak down here. Sacrifice yourself here in the minor leagues, prepare yourself mentally and physically. Prepare yourself in every area of the game. Then when you go there, you're going to understand what you have to do."

Tony Gwynn, San Diego's greatest star and one of the finest hitters in the majors, met Roberto that same spring.

"It seems like in spring training, everybody always congregates by the batting cage," he remembers. "At the time we had four cages — the guys from the major league side who liked to work extra at the cage, but the minor league guys were usually there first. We always had to get them to give up one cage while they used the other three. Guys like Robbie, Jerald Clark, Shane Mack were always getting their extra work in. That's where I ran across him and got a chance to talk to him and watch him hit. Robbie was real quiet then. He didn't have too much to say. He just went about his business, especially when the major league guys came over. I remember watching him hit. He had a real natural swing, real fluid, real to the point. And the ball just kind of jumped off his bat. With a young guy, you didn't see that — you might see that in a guy twenty-one or twenty-two. I remember asking him 'How old are you?' He said nineteen. I said, 'Gawd you've got good swing.' Then he told me he was a switch hitter, which really blew me away because a guy who swings that good, you just don't expect him to be a switch hitter. So we got to talking about which side was his power side and which was his contact side. We struck up a friendship from there."

While Robbie was turning heads, Sandy Sr. had caught an unexpected break. In 1986, Dick Williams, who had been managing the Padres, parted company with the team during spring training, leaving the organization in a quandary. Steve Boros, the team's minor league coordinator, was parachuted into the job and had to put together a coaching staff in a hurry. Normally, it would have taken Sandy several years to secure a job on the major league level. Instead, after just one year in A Ball, he was summoned to the big club to work with Boros. The Alomar family reunion had lasted only one year, but since both of the boys seemed destined for the majors, there was every reason to believe they would all wind up together eventually.

Roberto moved on to the Wichita Wranglers (formerly the Wichita Pilots) of the AA Texas League, along with Sandy Jr., for the 1987 season. His roommate in spring training was Carlos Baerga. "He taught me how to play, because he was a year ahead of me," Baerga says. "I have to give credit to his father, too, because he was the one that showed me how to be quick with my hands on the double play, and how to play defence. Robbie is like my brother. We used to always go out for a bite to eat. He liked to have fun. We'd go out to play pool, go eat together or watch a movie. We always liked to be doing something. We didn't want to sit in the room and get bored.

During the season, Roberto lived with his brother Sandy in Wichita. "We lived in a one-bedroom apartment. One day you sleep on the couch, one day you sleep on the bed. We switched. At that time I was making over a thousand a month. I remember we bought a car for like $300. The insurance was more expensive than the car." Roberto again put up fine numbers — .319, 68 RBIs, 43 stolen bases — but more significantly, he played shortstop regularly for the first time since he was fifteen years old. "They wanted me to play shortstop, because they didn't know if Garry Templeton would play with the team or if he would retire," Roberto says. "I didn't like shortstop that much, but in that situation it's not your decision. I played shortstop as a kid, but I always liked second base better. It's easier for me, it's a shorter throw. I was made to play second base. I wanted to follow in my Dad's footsteps. He played second so I wanted to play second because he was my idol."

The bright idea of Alomar moving to shortstop would surface again a few years later, with rather serious consequences. But in the minors, even though Roberto had no interest in being anything other than a second baseman, he wasn't complaining because things were unfolding just as his father had anticipated when he signed with the organization. One way or another, he was on the fast track to the major leagues, and that was all that really mattered.

It couldn't come quickly enough for Roberto, who found the minor league lifestyle not entirely to his liking. While major league ballplayers have a well-earned reputation for being pampered, and many earn salaries beyond the wildest dreams of the ordinary working stiff, the minor leagues are closer to what baseball used to be like. There, the players are workers, the perks are few and far between, and even the best prospects aren't getting rich.

"People say to me now, 'Roberto, you have everything.' When I used to play in the minors, we didn't have anything. We had to buy our own equipment. There are a lot of things in the life of a baseball player that people don't know. I only made $700 a month the first year. I don't know how much my brother and my dad made. And when we were away, we got an extra ten dollars a day in meal money. Even when I got to AA in Wichita, and I was making $1200 a month, it was still tough to live on that money. You eat McDonalds, pizza, whatever. And then there were the bus trips. Ten, twelve, fourteen hours. The worst ones were in AA — fifteen or sixteen hours on a bus when you were going from Wichita to El Paso. You got on the bus after the game and you got home the next day. Then you were so tired that you went to bed all day long. You had to go through all that pain to see if you could make it to the big leagues."

As it turned out, his pain in the minor leagues was remarkably short-lived. In 1988, both Alomar brothers went to spring training with the Padres, albeit with very different expectations. The year before, the Padres had fallen to sixth place in the National League West with a record of 65–97, 25 games off the pace — their worst finish in six years. One of the few bright spots, though, was catcher Benito Santiago, a fellow Puerto Rican who had been scouted and signed by Luis Rosa, and had been named National League rookie of the year. He was just twenty-three years old, and figured to have a lock on the Padres' catching job for as long he chose. Sandy Jr. knew the organization wouldn't likely keep him in the major leagues as a back-up, letting him watch from the bench while running up days of major league service that would go towards qualifying him for salary arbitration down the road. Barring a miracle, he was bound for the AAA Las Vegas Stars, and sooner or later either he or Santiago was bound for another team in a trade.

Roberto, though, didn't have anything close to that kind of obstacle in front of him. The leading candidates for San Diego's second base job that spring were veterans Randy Ready and Tim Flannery, neither of whom had really established themselves as starters at the major league level. Both of them were far more suited to a utility role. There were other young infielders in the system, but none ready to step in right away.

He was a kid, and he had only spent three years in the minor leagues, but still Roberto found himself with a realistic opportunity to jump all the way from AA to the big leagues — though how much of an opportunity it really was depended on who was doing the talking.

From the outset, Padres manager Larry Bowa was Alomar's biggest booster. He had been the manager for the disastrous 1987 campaign, and rightly figured his neck was on the line if the team didn't get off to a decent start in 1988. He wanted the best team possible on the field from opening day, and if that meant taking the risk of rushing Alomar to the big leagues rather than going with someone like Randy Ready, it was worth it.

"I haven't decided to send him down," Bowa said to reporters just a few days after the players reported. "Maybe some other people have."

The other people Bowa was referring were the powers in the Padres' front office, especially team president Chub Feeney. They weren't as worried about short-term success and they were clearly gun-shy about rushing Alomar to the majors. They could back up that feeling by citing recent Padre history — history that had nothing to do with whether Roberto Alomar was ready for the major leagues or not.

Second base had for some reason been a cursed position in San Diego. Once upon a time, Juan Bonilla looked like he'd be a fixture at second for the 1980s. But he broke his wrist, he never really came back from the injury, and then had drug problems. In 1984, Alan

Wiggins arrived after being drafted from the Dodgers as an outfielder. He was moved to second base, stole 70 bases and scored 106 runs. The Padres won their first and only pennant that year. Drugs then destroyed his career.

"It looked like we were set with Bonilla, then he faded, and then we lost Wiggins too," Jack McKeon said. "You lose two guys like that at such a key position and it sets the whole organization back."

Two years before Alomar arrived, in 1986, the Padres had brought up a can't-miss phenom from AA to step in as their starting second baseman. But Bip Roberts wasn't quite ready, he couldn't quite handle the pressure, and the experiment was judged a failure.

A year before, the Padres again brought up a can't-miss phenom from AA and made him their starting second baseman. But Joey Cora, a young Puerto Rican, also wasn't quite ready, he couldn't quite handle the pressure, and the experiment was judged a failure.

And so in the spring of 1988, the team's top brass was not exactly predisposed to taking chances with a young player, even if he did look like the best prospect in their entire minor league system — if not in the entire minor leagues. Bowa didn't feel that way, the other players didn't feel that way — they just wanted to win. Alomar, still naive about the politics of the game, thought with all his heart that he was ready to make the jump, and figured that if he played as well as he could, they would have no choice but to keep him.

Throughout spring training, the debate continued and intensified as Alomar performed better and better. On March 1, Bowa said that veteran Ready had the inside track on the starter's job, and that Cora was still in the picture. But the kid had a shot as well.

"Tell you what. He's the best-looking infielder I've seen in a long time. A lo-o-o-o-ong time. He can do some things. He's solid. There's no doubt in my mind that he can play second right now in the majors. We'll have to see about his hitting once the games start."

The Cactus League schedule began the next day with Alomar as the Padres' starting second baseman. He had seven hits in three games, and Bowa was impressed.

"Actions speak, and up until now, with Robbie, actions have spoken. I've seen kids like Ryne Sandberg in his first year, and as far as fundamentals are concerned, this kid is just as sound as Sandberg. You know what else tells me he's ready? He doesn't give a damn who is put out there pitching. He doesn't even know who is out there. He just plays. He might struggle in April and May, but when all the dust is settled, he is going to hit at least .250 and catch everything."

Which made it sound like Alomar had the job in the bag. He did not.

"Joey Cora, unfortunately, has become the forgotten man," Feeney explained. "That has to be part of your thinking. We don't want to rush somebody. No question Alomar has had a great spring. But guys have done that before. He's going to be a good player. But we have to evaluate just when."

Bowa remained steadfast in his opinion. "I know I've got the deck stacked against me with past history," he said. "But you've got to deal with each individual separately. You can't throw all rookies together. People are tricked when they see he's just twenty. He has played with major leaguers in Puerto Rico since he was sixteen years old. He has been around major league baseball for years with his father. Baseball-wise, he is really mature. I'm telling you, no matter how long we wait to bring him up here there is going to be an adjustment period. Every rookie has to go through it, no matter who they are. All I know is that if they send Alomar down, it's just a matter of time. A year, a year and a half, it doesn't matter. When he comes up, he'll be here to stay."

The players, by and large, agreed with their manager. "In his first big league camp, you could see it," Tony Gwynn says. "For a guy who wasn't given much chance to make the club, he just did it all. He'd turn the double play, he'd go in the hole, he'd make diving stops, he'd slide and throw a guy out at first, he'd steal bases. He did everything. From the first exhibition game we played until the last one before they sent him out, we all knew he was going to make the club. There was just no doubt he was going to make the club.

Alomar, whose play spoke for itself, was nonetheless drawn into the debate about whether he was ready to make the jump. "I want to try the big leagues," he said. "I've been playing a lot of A [spring training] games against big leaguers. I've seen them all my life. I think I'm ready. I try to be a smart hitter. I try to play hard and never give up."

Then there was Ready, who had just a teeny tiny bit of a vested interest in any decision. "I think Alomar is a good player," he said, "but they have to be careful. Their last two experiments haven't worked out. He has the potential to look good, but then a lot of kids look good now. I think experience has to play a big role. I've got that."

Alomar's performance didn't let up as spring training neared its conclusion. On March 21, he went 3–4 with a two-run homer off Rick Sutcliffe, and was riding an eight-game hitting streak. "I told him around the batting cage, 'You know, it's Sutcliffe today,'" said Gwynn. "He just said, 'He still has to throw the ball over the plate.' You expect that from a veteran, not from a twenty-year-old kid."

Dickie Thon, the fine Puerto Rican shortstop whose career was marred by a terrible beaning, was also trying to make the Padres' opening day roster that spring. "In 1988 I saw Roberto — he was very young and he was ready to play in the big leagues. Bowa was the manager and he wanted him on the team, but Feeney kept saying he wasn't ready. It was ridiculous because he hit about .400 and he played great."

"I know I'm putting pressure on them," Alomar said. "I'm not making their decision easier. But I told them if they put me in there, I'm going to play hard. I don't care where it is. I want to play. I don't want to sit on the bench."

By March 24, his spring training average sat at .357 (.415 in the past ten games) and he was making all the plays in the field. "With the spring I've had, I'm supposed to make it," Alomar said. "If I don't make it, what do I have to do to make it? Be a veteran? I know if it's up to Larry, I'll make it. But Chub Feeney is worried about it. If he only lets me in the big leagues, I'll show him. After a spring training like I've had, nobody is supposed to go to AAA."

Once they've had a taste of the majors, nobody wants to go back to AAA. Roberto had had enough of the bus rides, the meagre meal money, the minor league lifestyle. After just a hint of the big leagues — and all those years watching his father play in the majors — Roberto knew what he wanted and he wanted it now. "You go to a AAA field and a big league field — they're not the same. No way you want to go there after you play in a big league park. The ground is nice, the dirt. The clubhouse is much bigger. You have satellite TV. You have a weight room.

"In the minor leagues, you don't have any of that. It's just a little tiny clubhouse. Sometimes in A ball, you even have to dress in your room and wear your uniform to the ballpark. You come back with a uniform and give it to the trainer and he takes it to the laundry. Man, it's an entirely different way to live. In the big leagues, your uniform is right there. You have your own locker. And you go out and play ball. You play with more talented guys. You play with better umpires. You play in better stadiums. More people see you play. You get paid more, and you get more meal money. You don't suffer. You don't want to go back to the minor leagues. No way. Whenever you get to the big leagues, it's to stay in the big leagues. You don't ever want to go back."

Near the end of spring training, the Padres brain-trust gathered in a room at the Ray Kroc Complex to discuss the final cuts and the make-up of the major league team. One coach sat in the meetings and tried to be dispassionate, but that would go against nature. So instead, he just tried to be quiet.

"I didn't say much," Sandy Sr. says. "They laid out the pluses and minuses. I just tried to stay within reason with what I had to say. I felt like he could have stayed. But he would have been staying against the wishes of Feeney. And if anything had happened within a week or two weeks, if Robbie had struggled, they would have sent him down right away, and he would have stayed down longer."

"They really wanted him to go back to AAA," says San Diego baseball writer Barry Bloom. "It was part jerking him around on being eligible for arbitration, and it was part not really wanting him to jump from AA to the major leagues so quickly. They wanted him to play at least half a year in AAA."

"They're going to deny it," Gwynn says, "but the reason they sent him out was because at the time, you had to play six years before you could become a free agent. If they sent him out for a month and brought him back they'd have him basically for seven years. That's why they sent him out. Somebody asked me why I thought they'd sent him down, and I said well I think what they're doing is sending him out for a month and bringing him back and then they get to keep him for another year. That's what they did to me. Chub took offence at this and we got into it. But that's why they did it. And who can blame them? When you have a talent like that, why not keep him as long as you can?"

On the last day before rosters were set, Roberto was called into Bowa's office, where Feeney was also sitting, and told that he would be starting the season in Las Vegas, home of the Padres' AAA affiliate, the Stars. Publicly, he took the news reasonably well. "He didn't say much, except that he'd be back," Bloom remembers. Privately, he was devastated. He wept uncontrollably in the training room before regaining his composure enough to face his teammates and the press.

Gwynn remembers, "He couldn't take it. He didn't want to be in front of the players. He didn't want the other players to see him. When I found out that he got sent out, I went over and tried to talk to him. But everything I was saying didn't mean much because he knew he did everything. He did everything that they asked him to do. He did more than they asked him to do. He deserved to make the club and he didn't. I went over there and told him the standard stuff — hey, you'll be back, go down there with a good attitude and do your job and you'll be back. But you could tell it was just bouncing off of him. It didn't sink in or nothing. There isn't anything that anyone is going to tell you that is going to make any sense to you. There wasn't anything we could say to him. You try to console him, you try to explain to him how baseball works, you try to explain to him what we thought was happening. He didn't want to hear that."

"He was crying," Sandy Sr. remembers. "That was hard for all of us. He had a great spring. They felt like he was young and they didn't want him to go through the same thing that Joey Cora and Bip Roberts went through. They didn't realize what Larry realized — that Robbie was a different kind of guy because he was brought up in a different kind of way. He was brought up in the game. Larry knew that Robbie was a different kind of player. He was a different species.

"He should have been upset," Sandy Jr. says. "It broke my heart when I saw Robbie crying. He said, 'I can't believe they sent me down.' I really thought he had the team made."

"Everybody knew he should have made the team," says Thon. "But for some reason, that sometimes happens. They had told him that if he played well, he was going to make the club, and then he went out and did everything imaginable to make the team and he didn't make it. But he's strong. He got that from his father — a strong-minded guy."

Even Flannery, one of his rivals for the second base job, knew that an injustice had been done. "Robbie got a raw deal," he said. "But that's the nature of the business. I remember going into the trainer's room that day and just saying, 'Keep your head up. The right time will come for you. You're going to be playing a long, long time in the big leagues. You're not even going to remember this day.' " He was wrong about the last part.

"I had a great spring training, and I got sent down," Alomar says now, so matter-of-factly that it's hard to imagine he was ever disturbed by what happened. "I led the team in hitting. I led all of the categories. I was disappointed. But I was still young. I was only twenty years old."

Roberto packed his bags, left his team and headed across the Mojave Desert to Las Vegas. "When they sent him out, he was talking like he wouldn't go for a week," Gwynn says. "They tried to appease him by giving him a little bit of a raise on his AAA contract and he reported on time. But none of that stuff means a hill of beans when you know you should be in the big leagues." In Vegas, he moved into an apartment that Sandy Jr. was already sharing with Joey Cora.

"We said, why don't you just move in here and stay with us for a week?" Sandy Jr. says. "That's about how long you're going to be here."

5

 BIG LEAGUER

Sandy's estimate was just a little bit off. Nine games into the season, twenty-three days after Roberto had been sent down, the call came.

At that point, Robbie had already knocked in fourteen runs for the Las Vegas Stars. However upset he had been at being exiled to the minors, he at least hadn't done any sulking on the field. To do so would have violated his father's code of conduct. "Once Robbie put on the uniform, he was going to play," Sandy Sr. says. "He went over there and he just played as well as he could play."

While he was playing so well, it was becoming obvious to everyone involved with the Padres that Randy Ready wasn't going to be the answer at second base, even on a temporary basis. "It wasn't pre-ordained that Robbie would come back up," Sandy Sr. says. "But the guys that we had weren't playing well at second base. We just didn't have guys who were making double plays. They had no choice. We had a decent ballclub, but the guys were not doing the job the way they were expected to." With the Padres off to a slow start, and with his own job clearly on the line, manager Larry Bowa finally convinced his masters that it was worth taking a chance. Better to take the risk of rushing Alomar and have a chance at winning a few games than to go down the drain with Ready.

"I was in the Las Vegas clubhouse," Roberto remembers. "I was getting ready to go out and play, but I noticed that they hadn't put me in the lineup. I thought 'what's going on, why am I not playing?' Then they told me I was going to the big leagues. I waited until I got home before I phoned my family. My Dad was with San Diego, so he already knew, and he told my Mom, so she already knew. I packed my bag, then I left to join the team. The Padres were playing the Dodgers in Los Angeles, so I went there. The first three games were postponed by rain, so I didn't get to play. We went back to San Diego to open up a series with Houston."

"He came up," says Tony Gwynn, "with a big smile on his face."

The first game against the Astros was scheduled for April 22 at Jack Murphy Stadium. At twenty years and a bit more than two months old, Robbie was the youngest player in the major leagues. The pitcher due for his turn in Houston's starting rotation was one of the oldest, a fellow named Nolan Ryan.

And so the Alomar family baseball saga had come full circle. Ryan broke into the big leagues with the New York Mets in 1966, just two years after Sandy Sr. They had played against each other many times, and they were teammates with the California Angels. Like everyone else in baseball who had been around them, Ryan remembered watching the Alomar boys hanging around the clubhouse and playing ball whenever they could. Many times in California he had played with them, even teaching young Roberto how to pitch.

Now he would be pitching to one of them in a major league game, and now Roberto would be facing one of his childhood idols.

"It was great playing against Ryan," Roberto says. "It was weird because I was facing a guy who taught me how to pitch when I was a little kid. He always used to tease me about how he was the one who taught me how to pitch. You never thought he'd still be there at that age. That was great for me — playing against a guy that my Dad played. And it was nice to come out of the locker room and see all the people in the crowd. I wasn't nervous, though. I never get nervous. I just went out to have some fun. I never feel pressure. I never have felt pressure in the game. What's the pressure going to do for you? It's going to make you do worse. This is a fun game. I go there and have some fun. My heart will not pump. I just try to be as relaxed as I can."

When it was his turn to step to the plate, Roberto did his best to forget about the situation, forget who was pitching, forget who was watching, forget that this was finally it, the moment he had waited for since he was a little boy, his chance to play in the big leagues just like his dad. He filed away the emotions and let the baseball part of his brain take over. This was just another game, another situation to be analyzed, another pitcher trying to outsmart you. It was all second nature.

Sandy Sr. was coaching at third, and he too was trying to treat the situation as professionally as possible, even though this was his son batting for the first time in the major leagues against one of the greatest pitchers of all time. "Sure you get nervous," he admits. "I played with

Ryan, he pitched to me, and now he's pitching to my son. You want your kid to do well all the time. Deep down inside, you know that they will not do good every day. So I was nervous."

Roberto worked Ryan to a 2–2 count. "Then he threw me a curveball. It was a good one, but kind of hanging up on top of the plate. I hit it on the ground between shortstop and third base. The third baseman tried to make a good play on it, but he knew he couldn't throw me out. He caught it on the run, but he didn't even try to throw the ball because there was no way he could get me out."

"That," says Sandy Sr., "was a big thrill." The ball was of course retrieved and put aside and now it has a place in the trophy case in the house in Salinas, which these days is filled to bursting. (A few years later, when Roberto was with Toronto and Ryan with Texas, they would make a little more history together and provide another souvenir ball — this time for Ryan's no doubt extensive collection. Alomar struck out to complete Ryan's seventh career no-hitter.)

Roberto turned a gorgeous double play in the ninth inning of that game to preserve a Padres victory, and after that stepped into the starting second baseman's job as though he had been born to it, which of course in some ways he had. He loved playing for Bowa, in large part because Bowa was one of the people in the organization whose faith in him had never wavered. "Larry Bowa taught players the way people taught him to be," Robbie says. "He used to be yelled at by his manager, so he did the same to his players. I've had managers who said something to your face and something different behind your back. I don't mind if they yell to your face, as long as they say the same thing when you're not there. Bowa liked to play aggressive ball. If you didn't play hard for him, he was going to be tough on you. That's the way it's supposed to be. If you don't want to play hard for a guy then he's going to tell you. If you don't want to play then let somebody else play. Bowa always treated me good. He never yelled at me."

He never yelled because Alomar, like his father, understood the game, was a deferential organization man, and was also a rookie who knew his place in the team hierarchy. With players like Tony Gwynn in the clubhouse, Roberto wasn't a major presence within the team, at least off the field. He just watched, listened and did his job.

On April 30, he hit his first major league home run, and received a standing ovation from the San Diego fans. Almost immediately after that, he went into his first major league slump. Between May 7 and 20, he went 6–39 at the plate, dropping his average to .215. Bowa benched him for a game, and Robbie responded by coming back to drive in the winning run in the bottom of the ninth off reliever Kent Tekulve as the Padres beat the Philadelphia Phillies.

"I didn't feel pressure about my slump," Alomar said. "But that hit made me feel more happy. I saw Tekulve all the time when I was a kid. I knew he threw a lot of sinker balls, and I waited for him to bring the ball up."

A couple of days later — now swinging a hot bat, having gone 4–14 since his brief benching — Alomar gave his manager credit for being tough when he had to be. "I didn't want to sit down," he said. "But that made me think. Looking back, Larry was smart to sit me down. I needed it."

Bowa didn't mind hearing that he was right about something. His team was dead last, and he knew that someone was going to have to take the fall unless there was a dramatic turn-around, fast. "We had a good team, but the other teams were better than us," Roberto remembers. "We didn't have much pitching and we didn't have that much offensive power. We didn't score a lot of runs.

"Some of the players didn't like Bowa because he wanted everybody to play the game the way he played it — he wanted everybody to play hard. Some of the guys weren't hustling and he was saying so to their faces. That's just the way he was."

But Alomar's play, though sometimes erratic, was a bright spot for Bowa. He had pushed to get him to the majors, he had taken the heat during his first rookie slump, and now it looked as though Roberto was again prepared to excel.

"I'll tell you what," Bowa said to reporters on May 22. "One day, he will be a twenty-homer man. Maybe not this year, but one day." That prediction, which is still to be borne out, was one of Bowa's last utterances as manager of the San Diego Padres.

Baseball managers are hired and fired for a variety of different reasons, most of which have nothing to do with the strategic decisions that baseball writers and fans so love to analyze. Their task is a simple one: put the best players available on the field, don't do anything to lessen their chances of victory, a few times a year do something that actually leads to a win. But their task is also as complicated as the intricacies of human relationships. Like any boss, they have to deal with the full range of personalities, with egos and insecurities, and find a way for them to co-exist. They have to take a group of men between twenty and forty years of age, from a broad and diverse range of backgrounds —

ethnically, culturally, economically — and help them remain motivated throughout the longest season in professional sport. They have to gain respect from players who likely have far greater talent than they did when — and if — they played the game, and who may well be earning several times their salary.

They have a limited say in personnel decisions, but still if things go badly, they know the buck stops with them. They get fired because their players aren't good enough, because their players won't play for them, because their personal style isn't compatible with the style of the team. And every once in a while, it happens that a change at the top produces lasting harmony and production throughout the ranks. A prime example was the Blue Jays decision to replace the high-strung, defensive Jimy Williams with the very relaxed and fair-minded Cito Gaston.

Far more often, though, a team that's bad for one manager stays bad for another. The fans and the press can enjoy the ritual sacrifice, but in the end it doesn't amount to much.

Bowa had been on the job for a season plus two months when the axe fell, and the firing came to no one's surprise. In 1987, the club had finished sixth. In 1988, it was still in sixth. That might have been taken as a pretty good indication that there wasn't adequate talent on the field, but that's not an explanation that can be sold to ticket-buyers. Instead, it was time to replace a young, aggressive screamer of a manager with an older, laid back, let-the-players-play type of individual.

That Jack McKeon was already the team's general manager put a slightly different spin on it — these were the players he had acquired and signed, and if he couldn't win with them, he could probably expect dire consequences. But the basic equation was the same — subtract one guy, add another, and try to change the atmosphere, shake up the players, and then hope that somehow everyone is newly inspired in their work.

At fifty-eight, McKeon was fifteen years older than Bowa. Twice before he had been a field manager, with the Kansas City Royals from 1973 through 1975, and with the Oakland Athletics for part of 1977 and all of 1978, twice finishing second with the Royals, doing nothing with the As. He was a cigar-smoking old-time baseball man. From an Alomar point of view he was a fine choice. He had hired Sandy Sr. and signed Roberto and Sandy Jr. With McKeon at the helm, both of the Alomar brothers knew that they could expect a fair shake. And Sandy, as third base coach, soon found himself calling his own signals and having a major role in running the team on the field. (Chub Feeney, who had fought so hard to hold Roberto back, would last just a little bit longer than Bowa. On September 25, the day after he allegedly made an obscene gesture to a group of disenchanted fans in Jack Murphy Stadium who were holding up a "Scrub Chub" banner, he resigned as the team's president.)

"It was fun playing for Jack," Roberto says. "He was in love with the game. And he was a caring person. He cared about his players. An awful lot like Cito Gaston."

The honeymoon began immediately between the new manager and the players. McKeon's relaxed, positive style played well in the clubhouse. Without worrying whether they would be hollered at, whether a bad play would put them in the doghouse or on the bench, they could just go out and enjoy themselves on the field. They were a happy team and suddenly a winning team, and the winning only made them happier. And all because their new boss had managed to enhance everyone's self-esteem.

"Jack McKeon makes us feel wanted," pitcher Andy Hawkins explained at the height of the love-in. "He makes us enjoy the game and he's our biggest fan."

Roberto enjoyed playing for McKeon just as he had enjoyed playing for Bowa — he enjoyed playing, period, especially in the big leagues. But he was still a rookie, he was still twenty years old, and while the team found a groove, Alomar's performances remained inconsistent through the middle of the season. He seemed to be simply trying to do too much, especially in the field.

"He started real good and then he got down just a little bit," Sandy Sr. says. "He was trying to play a little bit too hard. Robbie was skinny then. Sometimes it seemed like he was overmatched. But Robbie's the type of kid that makes a lot of adjustments. He adjusts with the pitcher, he adjusts with the game, he adjusts with the people that he's playing with. That's just something that he has. I used to see the same thing with Tony Gwynn — he used to carry a VCR around with him all the time and used to watch his tapes every day. I know that the good players always try to watch what they're doing so they can make adjustments."

"This guy played for me in the big leagues when he was twenty years old," McKeon says. "And God almighty, he didn't need a third base coach. You'd better be awake when he's out there, because if you happen to go to sleep, you might get hit with the ball because it's coming to you. He's a tremendously gifted athlete. Tremendous.

"But when he first came up, people in San Diego got on him. They said he was careless. But that was just immaturity. That was mental discipline that he was acquiring but that he just hadn't put all together. When you're a twenty-year-old kid in the big leagues, your mind wanders a bit. But there wasn't anything that wasn't going to be corrected by another year of playing."

"I think most of his problem was that they were right about the instructional part of going from AA to the major leagues," says baseball writer Barry Bloom. "He was trying to do too much too soon. But unlike Benito Santiago, who became indignant when you pointed out that he had made a mistake, Robbie was a quick study. If you pointed out to him that he did something wrong, he always tried to eliminate what he was doing. On most of his errors, he was going after balls, diving up the middle to catch a ball that he shouldn't have been able to get to in the first place, then instead of holding onto it because he wasn't going to get the baserunner, just throwing it into centrefield. A lot of it wasn't stupid errors. It was a combination of inexperience and not really knowing how to control his abilities in the major leagues."

"People were kind of criticizing Robbie for being lackadaisical in the way he played," Gwynn says. "We'd get on him all the time about the routine play. The press and the fans used to give Robbie a hard time with that too. If there was a groundball up the middle, instead of trying to get in front of it, he would field it to the side and flip it to first instead of planting and throwing. It almost looked like he was being nonchalant. But that's just his style, that's the way he played it. But Robbie didn't like it very much when the fans or media got on him."

After the All Star break in 1988, it appeared corrections were already starting to take place. Roberto hit

.316 in the last fifty-five games of the season, made only four errors in the last sixty-four, had three hitting streaks of at least ten games in August and September, ended up leading the team in runs scored, doubles and sacrifices and was voted the Padres' rookie of the year. The club that was 16–30 when Bowa was fired went 67–48 under McKeon, finishing in third place, 11 games out. The future for the franchise looked bright, moving McKeon into the dugout looked like an act of genius. Whatever other adjustments would have to be made in the off season, second base appeared set for a long time to come — though of course the Padres had thought the same thing a few times before.

"It would seem that the Padres have the second baseman who will take them into and through the 1990s," Dave Distel wrote in the Los Angeles *Times*, "but no one is making such outrageous and sensible predictions. After all, second base on this team is not a position, but rather an insatiable monster that devours its young."

Spring training in 1989 figured to be entirely different from the year before. Robbie signed a new contract that paid him $155,000 a season — close to what the former rookie of the year Santiago had earned the year before. And from the first day of camp, the second base job was his. "Last year I had to come here and try to make the team," he said. "You have to do everything, and sometimes you try to do too much. Now I am here, I have to do the best I can. I don't have to make the team, but I have to work hard. When I first came here, I never thought about what happened to Joey [Cora] and what happened to Bip [Roberts]. I just came here to win the position."

On opening day, Roberto was still the youngest player in any lineup in the major leagues, but instead of being part of a team with relatively low expectations, he was now an integral part of a squad that thought it might have a shot at a division title.

As the season progressed, the Padres continued to look like contenders, and Alomar continued to look like a rising star. But in the field, especially early in the season, he was still making enough errors to draw heat from the local press, and occasionally from the fans.

"I'm not afraid to make mistakes," Roberto says. "I'm going to go out there and try to make every play that I can make. The problem was that I didn't have too much sense of the game. Sometimes you have to read the play before it happens. At that time I was still young. Every day I learned more and more. I made a lot of mistakes because instead of holding the ball I threw it. Sometimes you have to realize who is running, who is not running, who can run, who can't run. Sometimes when they hit the ball to my side, I have to just put it in my pocket. I charged balls that I shouldn't have charged — I should have stayed back and thrown the ball to first base. I'd go for the ball instead of staying back. But I learned making the mistakes. That's the way it is with a human being. The thing about this game is that you can learn a lot from the bad things.

"When you make a lot of errors, they're going to talk about your defence," he continues. "If you don't make a lot of errors, they're not going to talk about your defence. You have to be prepared for the media and prepared for everybody whenever you do badly. I was the same guy when I was doing badly or when I was doing well."

Meanwhile, Sandy Jr.'s professional career was taking a very different path. His first years in the minor leagues had been a struggle, especially as a hitter, and some people in baseball were sceptical about whether he would ever develop his raw tools into the stuff of a major league catcher. It wasn't until 1987 that his true potential began to emerge.

"They sent me back to AA in 1987 and that was really the turning point in my career, because I had a great year," Sandy says. "That's when they started thinking good about me. They sent me to AAA in 1988, and I had an outstanding year." He was so outstanding, in fact, that *Baseball America* named him the AAA player of the year after he hit .297 with 16 home runs and 71 runs batted in. "But I was caught behind Benito Santiago, and they couldn't trade me, so I came back to AAA in 1989 and had an even better year."

Santiago had come into the major leagues with a bang and immediately established himself as the Padres starting catcher of the present and future. San Diego was left in an enviable position. Catchers are one of the most rare and valued commodities in baseball — especially young, defensively talented catchers who can swing a bat. There is such a shortage of talent that a decent defensive catcher can get to the majors without really being able to hit, and a position player with a decent bat (like Ed Sprague) will sometimes be converted to work behind the plate. The Padres, on the other hand, just happened to have two of the best young catchers to come along in years, who just happened to have grown up a few miles apart in Puerto Rico. Obviously, the team wasn't big enough for the both of them.

"Benito and I knew that we both were starting catchers and that somebody had to go," Sandy Jr. says. "I thought it was going to be me because he was an All Star, he was rookie of the year, he was already established in the big leagues. I didn't think San Diego was going to gamble with another rookie catcher and let a proven player go. I believed that another team would take me because of my low salary. I thought teams would be looking for a young catcher with a low salary to build a team around. And everything proved to be right."

In his role as vice president of baseball operations, it was up to McKeon to make the most of the situation. From the time Sandy started to develop in the minors, he knew that sooner or later a deal would have to be struck.

"I kept them together as much as I could. And I would have kept them all together except for the fact that I had two All Star catchers," McKeon says. "There ain't no way I can justify that. So this was almost an ironic case where you traded a guy for his sake and not for my sake. People in the business wanted the young kid. Benny had already been two years and won a gold glove and was an All Star, and so they knew that it was going to cost them money if they got him. It's better to take a chance on a rookie. You have three years before you even have to worry about arbitration. You get a club like Cleveland that's money-conscious, that's trying to keep the salary costs down, and it's an ideal situation. Everything worked in Sandy Jr.'s favour. And I thought I was doing him a favour by trading him and giving him a chance to develop his own credentials."

On December 6, 1989, Sandy Alomar, Carlos Baerga and Chris James were traded by the Padres to the Cleveland Indians in return for Joe Carter. It was a deal of enormous significance for both franchises. Alomar would become Cleveland's starting catcher. Baerga, yet another second baseman from Puerto Rico, would emerge as an enormous talent who drew comparisons to Roberto. Not everyone in baseball would be overjoyed at the prospect of playing for Cleveland — years of bad management, minuscule fan support and a huge, crumbling, usually empty stadium had long earned the Indians the reputation as the worst franchise in baseball. But for Sandy and Baerga, it was the perfect opportunity — they would get a chance to play, they would be part of a well-thought-out youth movement, they could grow with the team.

"It was incredible," Sandy Jr. remembers. "I was so happy I jumped three feet in the air. I was hearing all these rumours that I would be going to Atlanta, Philadelphia, and then nothing. When Jack McKeon called me and said, 'I'm very sorry, we've traded you to the Cleveland Indians,' I said, 'Man, don't be sorry. You've done me the greatest favour in my life.' I was so happy I don't think I slept for two or three days."

"I felt happy for him, because Benito was over there," Maria Alomar says. "'You have a chance now,' I told him. It was hard for me, because I was with Sandy Sr. in San Diego, and so I might not get to see him a lot of the time. But still I felt happy."

For Carter, it was the second time in his major league career that he had been involved in a blockbuster trade. In 1984, the Chicago Cubs, on their way to a division pennant, traded Carter, Mel Hall and Darryl Banks for Rick Sutcliffe, Ron Hassey and George Frazier. Even though Cleveland could be a dispiriting place to play, Carter had blossomed into one of the game's most consistent run producers with the Indians. In the previous four seasons, he had driven in 121, 106, 98 and 105 runs.

San Diego suited him just fine. It was a nice place to move his family, and the franchise was apparently on the verge of something big. "I was happy to get to San Diego," Carter remembers. "It was a chance to get out of Cleveland. It was a chance for me to play for a contending team and to play with a guy like Tony Gwynn."

During spring training in 1990, Carter first saw Roberto Alomar in action. "I first got wind of Robbie in an exhibition game that I think we were playing against the Angels," he remembers. "I had heard about who Robbie Alomar was, but I'd never really seen him too much. But that first game he got three or four hits, he was stealing bases, diving, making great plays. I looked at Tony Gwynn and said, 'Is this guy for real?' Tony said, 'Hey, this guy's going to get better. He's everything you see and more.' From that day forth, I said this guy's got a lot of potential. He can be a great ballplayer.

"On the field, Robbie made a lot of young mistakes," Carter says. "Getting thrown out stealing bases when the pitcher was in trouble — things like that. He didn't know when to run all the time. It was a matter of him running just to be running, and not knowing the situations. When some situation came up where he was thrown out, I would talk to him about it, mainly because I was hitting behind him. If he gets thrown out with me and Jack Clark coming up to the plate, that's a wasted effort on his part. I let him know that every now and then. But mainly it was just a matter of letting him get out there and play. He was just learning the game. But you could see that he had loads and loads of talent because he could go into rightfield and take away base hits, or up the middle. There was no limit to what he could do. I think he tried to hit a few more home runs than he normally would have tried to, but that all comes with maturity. That was something that he didn't have at that time. But he was already one heckuva ballplayer in 1990."

THE TURNING POINT: Roberto celebrates his home run off Dennis Eckersley in game four of the ALCS against Oakland. For the Blue Jays, it was a turning point in the 1992 playoffs.

SYSTEM 4 LIMITED

WATCHING: Wearing his trademark white headband and a pair of reflective shades, Robbie sits in the Blue Jays' dugout.

SYSTEM 4 LIMITED

BROTHERS: Robbie and Sandy Jr. get together before a Blue Jays-Indians game at the SkyDome.

FULL EXTENSION: Roberto dives to make a catch during his first season as a Blue Jay — 1991 — the kind of play that quickly endeared him to the Toronto fans.

TURNING THE DOUBLE PLAY: One of the most complex plays in baseball, and one of the real tests of any second baseman. The pivot requires teamwork, perfect position and quick thinking, all with the runner bearing down on you.

HIGH SKY: Robbie before an afternoon game at SkyDome with the roof open.
The eye black is the traditional method of cutting the sun's glare.

THE BOSS: Roberto talks with Cito Gaston and California Angels' manager Buck Rogers before a game at the SkyDome. "One of the toughest jobs in baseball is being a manager. I don't want to ever be in that spot."

SOCIALIZING: "It's very important for players – especially Latin players – to associate with the people. I go and talk to the people. If you don't talk to people, they're not going to get to know you."

YANKEES: Sandy Jr., Maria, seven-year-old Robbie, Sandy Sr. and Sandia in 1975, during Dad's playing days with New York.

HEROES: Sandy Sr., Robbie, Sandy Jr. and home run king Hank Aaron, then finishing his career with the Milwaukee Brewers, before a game in 1975.

PINSTRIPES: Robbie in Yankee uniform, 1974.
"My dad or my mother never told me what to do.
You're going to be what you want to be, they said.
I said, I'm going to play baseball."

ALL STARS: Roberto and Sandy Jr., both voted in as starters by the fans for the All Star Game in Toronto, 1991.

RELAXING: Roberto and Joe Carter share a joke before a game at the SkyDome during the 1992 season.

CHAMPIONS: Robbie and Juan Guzman celebrate the
Blue Jays victory in game six of the World Series in the
Toronto dressing room at Atlanta's Fulton County Stadium.

GREAT PLAY: Robbie congratulates veteran shortstop Alfredo Griffin
on a nice bit of fielding during the 1992 season.

MOTHER LOVE: Maria with her infant second son.
"My mom was always around. She never left us alone."

BOYS WILL BE BOYS: Sandy Jr. — the one with the antennae — and
10-year-old Robbie. "My brother is a real fun guy."

SUMMERTIME: Robbie,
10, piggybacking on Sandy
Jr. at one of their summer
homes in the U.S. "He used
to be more outgoing than
me. He could speak Eng-
lish real well. He used to go
out and make friends and
I'd follow him."

ALOMAR COLLECTION

HAPPY BIRTHDAY: Roberto's fifth birthday party. Note the baseball motif on the cake. "I always talked about baseball, baseball."

THE BRONX ZOO: Sandy Jr., "Superman" Sandy Sr., Jim "Catfish" Hunter, Robbie and Billy Martin in 1976.

ALOMAR vs ALOMAR: Robbie slides home as Sandy Jr. waits for a throw during an exhibition game between the Padres and their Triple A affiliate, the Las Vegas Stars.

DAD AT WORK: Coach Sandy Alomar Sr. focuses on the game. "My dad is a big influence on me because he used to play the game. I always wanted to be like him."

SECOND YEAR: The Padres team picture. Sandy Jr. is featured, though he didn't stick with the team. He would be traded to Cleveland during the off-season.

IN THE BIG LEAGUES: Robbie, with moustache, during his first season
with the San Diego Padres, 1988.

6

 DETOUR

On July 11, at the end of a streak during which the Padres lost fourteen of nineteen games, Jack McKeon stepped down as the Padres' field manager to concentrate on his duties as the team's vice president of baseball operations. Greg Riddoch was named as his replacement for the remainder of the season.

With that management shuffle, Sandy Alomar Sr. figured that, at least as far as his career with the San Diego Padres was concerned, the writing was on the wall. "I thought," he says, "that my future was gone."

Riddoch had been an All-American shortstop at Northern Colorado University in 1967, and was drafted four times by the Baltimore Orioles before finally signing with Cincinnati, who drafted him after his graduation from college. He never made it as far as the major leagues as a player, and eventually moved into a number of front office jobs for the Reds, including Scouting Supervisor and Director of Minor League Clubs.

He also managed in the Reds minor league system for eight seasons, beginning in 1974, winning two titles in the Northwest League. He joined the Padres organization in 1986, replacing Steve Boros as Director of Minor League Instruction when Boros took over the Padres from Dick Williams during spring training. That was the same shuffle that resulted in Sandy Sr. securing a coaching job in the major leagues.

In 1987, Riddoch joined the Padres as a dugout coach under Larry Bowa, and then became first base coach in 1988. In May 1989, two months before taking over, he moved back into the dugout to help manage the game from the bench.

During that time Sandy Alomar Sr., who knew something of clubhouse politics after all his years in the big leagues, found himself becoming less and less fond of the way Riddoch operated.

"When he first came to the team, Larry Bowa was there, and Larry was always with me, always talking to me. Riddoch was always sticking to me and Larry. We were always going out to have lunch or dinner. It seemed to me like he was the type of person that would try to get close to the person that was closest to the person above. That's the type of game he played. Then after Larry Bowa left, he got closer to me because he thought I was close to Jack McKeon. But I didn't really want to hang out. I'm a loner. I don't dislike people, but I just go to the ballpark to do a job. I get to the ballpark early. I leave the ballpark late. I do what I have to do.

"Then when [pitching coach] Pat Dobson got close to Jack — Dobson wanted to manage, too — Riddoch started leaving me and getting close to Pat. Everything was with Pat after that. Then, when he felt Pat wasn't going to get a job managing and McKeon was going down, he got close to [the team's chairman and managing partner] Tom Werner. He got close to Tom Werner, McKeon got fired, he got the job."

If that wasn't enough to sour him on his new boss, Riddoch's relationship with his son certainly did. Roberto had played for many different types of managers in the minors and pros, just as Sandy had run the gamut during his playing career. Both of them made it a point not to question authority. They did their jobs honestly, and expected to be treated honestly in return.

With Greg Riddoch, though, Robbie felt that trust was broken. Though it wasn't particularly obvious to outsiders as the season progressed, Alomar had a major falling out with his manager very early in Riddoch's tenure, and the rift never really healed. Two incidents had much to do with destroying their relationship.

During a series in Chicago, Riddoch decided that Roberto hadn't shown sufficient hustle in running out a groundball. After the game, he called him into his office, where the two had a closed door meeting. "He said, 'I hope this will stay between you and me,'" Roberto remembers. "Then the next thing I see there's something about it in the papers. That's what I didn't like about him. He would say something in the front and then something different in the back. Afterwards, I just showed him the paper. I didn't have to say anything else. I showed him the paper and I walked away. It's not supposed to be that way.

"I go out there and do my job. I was just letting him know that I wanted to play the game. Just because I didn't run once, he didn't have to punish me for that. There's a lot of guys that don't run sometimes. I made a mistake and I paid for my mistake. But all you have to do is tell me — don't tell the media. You have to trust somebody to play for him. You cannot put pressure on yourself if you do not trust somebody. When you play with something on your mind, you don't do your best. This guy is saying this, this guy is saying that, then players start talking about each other. That's not good."

"Riddoch was saying some things about him in the press, making it look like he had personal problems," Sandy Sr. says. "One time he asked him a question as though he had a family problem. Or as if he had a mental problem. How can he ask that when I was coaching for him? He didn't see any mental problem. Then he was saying to the press that Robbie's head wasn't in the game. His head was here. But Robbie was young and things like that started to bother him. I talked to Robbie and tried to make him understand. The guy was doing it but he wasn't trying to do any real harm to him. He was just trying to do something that he thought he had to do with the press. But it did bother me, because he knew that I was coaching for him, he knew that we didn't have any type of family problems. But I'm not the kind of guy that's going to go over to him and ask him, 'Why are you saying this?'"

"It wasn't just Robbie," Sandy Sr. continues. "A lot of players were feeling uncomfortable playing for him. Everything was negative. It seemed like he was two-faced. He was one thing when he was talking to you and he was another thing after you left."

The other troubling times for the Alomars were actually initiated by Jack McKeon before he gave up the manager's job, and could be traced back to some deep-thinking within the Padres organization when Roberto was playing in Wichita in 1987.

In late June, McKeon decided to make a radical change in his everyday lineup. Garry Templeton, who had been the team's shortstop for the past eight-and-a-half seasons — since he arrived in a trade for Ozzie Smith — was banished to the bench. Roberto Alomar was inserted in his place. Bip Roberts took over Alomar's job at second.

"It's still baseball. I don't think it will be that hard for me to do," Alomar said after his first game at shortstop since his stint in Wichita in 1987. "I played shortstop growing up, and once you play it, you don't forget. The only reason I moved to second was because I wanted to be like my dad. He was my idol, and I wanted to be just like him."

"I think he'll do well there," Sandy Sr. said. "He can handle it. Everything is how people want to accept it. It's kind of ironic — when I came up, I was a shortstop. Then they moved me to second."

Privately, the Alomars weren't feeling nearly so magnanimous about the move. Roberto, though he was still making a lot of errors, was looking more and more like one of the best second basemen in the game. In order to solve their problem at shortstop — at age thirty-four, Templeton's range was reduced dramatically — they created a problem where there hadn't been one and wouldn't be one. It was as if the Chicago Cubs had moved Ryne Sandberg to shortstop because whoever they had there wasn't doing the job. The San Diego braintrust thought that either Bip Roberts or Joey Cora would eventually step in and become at least an adequate defensive second baseman, but in the process they only increased Alomar's level of disenchantment with the team.

"They were trying to move Robbie from second to short," Sandy Jr. says. "Why would you want to mess around with an All Star second baseman? You fill a hole and create another hole."

"Jack put me in at short just because Garry was hurt and they wanted to try me," Roberto says. "I told him, I can try. I don't know if I can change because second base is my position. They were concerned because they didn't know if Templeton was going to stay in the game or if he was going to retire. I said I will try, but I didn't like it that much. I played a few games. I played well but I didn't like it."

After Roberto had played those few games at shortstop, baseball paused for the All Star break and McKeon stepped down. The 1990 All Star Game was played at Wrigley Field in Chicago, and for the first time, Roberto had been selected to play for the National League, while Sandy Jr., in the midst of his rookie-of-the-year season in Cleveland, was voted into the starting lineup for the American League by the fans. The Alomars became the first Latin American brothers to play together in the All Star Game.

"That was very special," Sandy Sr. says. "Having your two boys there, my being fortunate enough to be invited. Being in the game, playing the game, and then having your two boys doing it. People talking the way they were about them. I felt like it was one of the greatest things that ever happened to us — as a family, for my wife as a mother, and for my daughter. It's hard to describe what it meant. We're very proud of them. Anybody that has a kid will be proud of that kid when he accomplishes something.

"It was especially fun to have one on one team and one on the other. I wanted both of them to do well, of course. But I was with the National League so I wanted the National League to win."

"It was great," Roberto remembers. "I was with my dad and my brother was on the other side. I had one at-bat against Dennis Eckersley. I hit a line drive to left-centre, and the centrefielder caught it. I had fun with a lot of guys. I didn't get a lot of playing time because it was played in Chicago and Ryne Sandberg was there. So I spent more time watching my brother."

When he returned to the Padres, the shift to short-stop immediately became an issue, and Roberto asked for a meeting with Riddoch — behind closed doors — where he told him how he felt. "I told him I didn't want to play shortstop. I wanted to play second base," Alomar says. That was that, the experiment ended, Riddoch told the press that Alomar would be back at second for the remainder of the season.

But the rift between Riddoch and Roberto would remain, and the issue wouldn't really ever go away. In the end, it was San Diego's desire to find someone to play shortstop that would lead to Roberto's eventual departure from the Padres.

Riddoch's managerial style didn't exactly ignite the team. Under McKeon in 1990, they had gone 37–43. Under Riddoch for the remainder of the season, they went 38–44. Alomar, though, had a fine second half of the season. After committing thirteen errors before the All Star break, he had only five afterwards. And despite missing fourteen of the last twenty-four games with an elbow injury, he finished with a career-high 60 RBIs and a .287 average. "We had a good team there," Roberto says. "The year before we had finished second. They were trying to build and to win. We just didn't come through. The pitching was kind of short. A lot of people got hurt, the bullpen got hurt, and we went down to the minor leagues for replacements, but the pitching there wasn't strong enough. But at least they were trying to put a team together to win."

"We felt the team wasn't that far off," Carter says. "We finished in fourth place mainly because we played bad baseball. Maybe we were one pitcher short. We didn't have a consistent closer and a middle relief guy. Other than that we had all the ingredients of a championship ball club."

Late in the season, the Padres management showed what direction they planned to follow for the immediate future. On August 24, the team announced that Riddoch would stay on as manager for the 1991 season.

Sandy knew immediately what that meant. His relationship with Riddoch had continued to deteriorate as the season progressed. Next year, with Riddoch confirmed as manager, he would likely have the option of hiring his own coaching staff. Sandy figured, rightly, that he wouldn't be part of that.

"First he started saying all those stories about Robbie," Sandy says. "Then, when he used to go out with the other coaches, he didn't invite me. They used to have early workouts. Sometimes they didn't tell me. He knew that I was always early at the ballpark. He knew that I was the guy in charge of fixing the balls. They didn't tell me about the early workouts. I was a pro. I knew that. So one time, we had a workout in Philadelphia and he was trying to tell me he didn't know where I was. He knew very well that I was always in my room. I didn't go anywhere. I went from the room to the restaurant to the ballpark all the time, and then from the ballpark to my room. So I went over to him and I said, 'What was this? A secret?' Then he once tried to tell me that I was telling Robbie and Benny Santiago what was happening with the ballclub. I said, 'Come on, man. I'm a professional.' Whenever I have something to say to someone, I say it to his face. He didn't want me to talk to other teams about a job. He kept telling me that he didn't have anything to do with the front office. But I knew I was gone."

On September 21, the Padres fired McKeon from his job as vice president, the beginning of a purge that would end with thirty-one team employees fired, most of whom, like Sandy, had originally been hired by McKeon. The Padres had new ownership — the Tom Werner group taking over from the family of the late Ray Kroc — and with that came the belief that a major housecleaning was in order. "We believe that the Padres have the nucleus of a championship club," the statement from the team's new ownership group read. "But we also believe that, as we look at the decade ahead, a change in the front office is necessary to strengthen ourselves for the future." On October 2, Joe McIlvaine, who had been the vice president of baseball operations for the New York Mets, was hired as McKeon's replacement. He signed a five-year deal worth $1.6 million.

"There was a whole bunch of turmoil going on with the team," Tony Gwynn says. "When McIlvaine came in and people told him what was going on, he had to clean house. All he had to go by was what people told him. It looked like they were getting our house in order, at least until they made that deal."

The season dragged to a conclusion. In early September, Roberto had sprained ligaments in his left elbow in a collision covering first on a bunt attempt. The injury forced him out of the lineup for fourteen games and hampered his performance. On the last day of the season, Sandy Sr. was still unsure of his status with the team. He wasn't told that he wouldn't be back, and so he proceeded on the assumption that he would — packing up with Maria and moving back to Puerto Rico.

It was there later in October, at a point when he had little opportunity to find another job for the next season, that he was telephoned and told he'd been fired. He had left his baseball belongings in San Diego — he had to fly all the way back, pack them up, and then return home.

"Robbie was angry," Sandy says. "But I was already here in Puerto Rico and Robbie was over there in San Diego. He was mad not because I was fired — we have prepared our kids for all of that. They understand that this is a business, that this is a job that I have. He was mad because of the way I was fired. He felt like I wasn't given a chance to hook up with another team. That's the only reason he was mad."

Now, only one of the three Alomars remained in San Diego, and as far as Roberto knew, he would be staying there. He was assured by both Riddoch and McIlvaine that they had no interest in trading him. He bought his first house (he had tried to buy one in Salinas, right next door to his parents, in 1989, but he had been too young to sign the papers) and prepared to settle down in Southern California. Roberto wasn't happy about Riddoch, he wasn't happy about the way the organization had treated his father and he didn't believe Riddoch's protests that it was McIlvaine and not him who had wanted to get rid of Sandy Sr. But as a professional, he knew his job would be to return the next spring and give the team his best, no matter what the circumstances.

It wouldn't quite work out that way.

"We went into the winter thinking that Roberto was going to play shortstop for us the next season," Gwynn says. "Then Sandy was fired, and I could never understand the rift that developed at that point. Somebody in our organization felt like Robbie wasn't going to be able to play at the level he played at when his dad was here. I don't know where that came from. I don't know who said it, but obviously somebody in the organization felt like that."

In November, 1990, the major league general managers gathered for their annual meeting in Phoenix, one of the prime opportunities for baseball men to get together, socialize, and talk trades. The process is a bit like playing poker — you don't show your hand too early, you bluff and raise the stakes, and at any time you can fold and walk away from the table. You don't want to seem too anxious or too desperate, and you don't want other people to completely understand your agenda. You want to unload your problems and fill your holes, calculating all the time who might be ready to make the jump from the minors, who will be leaving through free agency, and who might be available on the open market.

Toronto's vice president of baseball, Pat Gillick, went to the meetings knowing that he still had the nucleus of a very good team. The Blue Jays had won the American League East in 1989, but in 1990 fell short of the division-champion Boston Red Sox. Their pitching staff was anchored by Dave Stieb, coming off an 18-win season, and their offence was keyed by Kelly Gruber, who had driven in a career-high 118 runs, outfielder George Bell, and first baseman Fred McGriff, who had hit 35 home runs. John Olerud had jumped straight from the college ranks to the big leagues, spending most of his time as designated hitter. Down the road, his position would be first base.

Gillick didn't necessarily enter the off-season looking to make wholesale changes, but he did know that one vacancy would have to be filled. George Bell had finally worn out his welcome, and would be headed elsewhere through free agency. "We knew we were losing him," Gillick says, "and we needed a righthanded hitter."

One of the people Gillick talked to in Phoenix was San Diego vice president Joe McIlvaine. Gillick had dealt with McIlvaine before when Joe held the same position for the New York Mets. Gillick asked whether Joe Carter might be available, but the discussion went nowhere. Roberto Alomar's name never came up.

"We never really thought there would be any opportunity to get him," Gillick says, "because his dad was up there."

A month later, at baseball's winter meetings, Gillick and McIlvaine talked again. By then, the Padres knew that they wouldn't have Jack Clark back in 1991, and so they were in the market for a first baseman. McIlvaine asked about McGriff, Gillick again brought up Carter, and a one-for-one deal was all but completed.

Then Gillick decided to play a wild card. "They had let Sandy go at that point," he says, "and we understood there was some friction between Roberto and Riddoch."

"If we talk McGriff and we talk Tony Fernandez," Gillick said to McIlvaine, "would you talk Alomar?"

Fernandez was the Jays' gifted shortstop from the Dominican Republic, a player who, though his career had been marred by injuries, remained one of the premier infielders in the game. What Gillick knew — and what McIlvaine didn't know — was that Fernandez had been making noises about leaving baseball altogether. A deeply religious man, he had told the Toronto management several times that he planned to retire when his contract expired to devote himself full time to his faith. "It wasn't a threat," Gillick says, "but it was just something that he had said too many times to disregard."

The Padres, who still desperately wanted to fill their hole at shortstop, were surprised but definitely intrigued by Gillick's proposition. Their thinking went something like this: we know Templeton is finished; we have Bip Roberts, who can play second base, and we have Joey Cora if Roberts doesn't work out; Fernandez is a great shortstop; having Fernandez at short playing with Roberts is better than having Alomar play second beside a terrible shortstop. "McIlvaine had hardly seen Alomar play," Barry Bloom says. "He didn't really know what he was giving up."

It didn't take long before McIlvaine was ready to strike the deal: Carter and Alomar for Fernandez and McGriff, four starters, four stars, a true blockbuster.

But Gillick temporarily put the brakes on. He wanted to confer with the rest of the Blue Jays braintrust. "We just wanted to have a look at the club when you put Carter and Alomar on it." They had Olerud to play first, they had an opening in the outfield for Carter, his RBIs would replace Bell's RBIs, Manuel Lee could move from second base to shortstop, his natural position. And they would add a young player who was already among the game's elite at his position and who had the potential to blossom into something more.

Still, Gillick came back to the table and tried to get just a little more of an edge. He asked McIlvaine to expand the deal. The Jays wanted San Diego pitcher Greg Harris. They would give up a player or two in return.

McIlvaine wasn't interested. "Joe said, 'We're prepared to do the two for two.'" And so the trade was made, the biggest in the history of either franchise. The players would be told first, and then it would be made public. The sports media in both cities would live off it for days, the fans went into shock.

No one would be more surprised than at least one of the principals.

"I was sleeping," Roberto remembers. "It was ten or eleven in the morning. My agent called me and told me, 'Sit down, relax.' I said, 'What's going on?' He said, 'You've been traded to the Toronto Blue Jays.' I said 'Whaaaat? For who?' he told me for Tony Fernandez and Fred McGriff — you and Joe Carter. After that, I turned the TV on and watched on the news about it. The media came to my house, the TV stations, and everybody. After that I talked to Joe. He was kind of upset because of his family. He had a house and I had just bought a house in San Diego. His kids and Tony Gwynn's kids were real close. He just put his kids in school. And then, after they had told him he would not get traded, he was traded. ("I told him it was a great city," Carter says, "and a great baseball town. Plus, they've got the SkyDome, so there's no problem with the weather — it's the same every day.")

"I knew I was moving onto a good team, a winning team, and to a place where the fans supported the team. I knew it was going to be good, but I didn't know how good it was going to be. I thought I was going to have to go there and replace Tony Fernandez. He played so well in that city. I didn't know how well I would play there and how I would adjust to the league and to the city. I didn't know anything about Toronto. I'd never been to Toronto. I never watched Toronto play, except against Kansas City in the 1985 playoffs. I'd never thought about being traded to Toronto. But life goes on. There's nothing you can do about it."

That's how Roberto, looking back, remembers his reaction to the trade. Then, the emotions were much, much stronger. When he heard the news, he wept, and he kept on crying, even as friends and family tried to console him.

"They told him that he was not going to be traded," Sandy Sr. says. "That's what McIlvaine told him. That's what Joe Carter said McIlvaine told him, too — that he was going to be there for a long time. So everybody was surprised. I didn't think they would trade him. The guy had had a great year, and every year he was getting better. He was growing as a person. All they needed was a shortstop to have a complete team. But it seemed like they just wanted to get rid of all of McKeon's people, and they did.

"Robbie phoned me here, and he was crying. I told him 'Robbie, you never know, maybe it's for the best. If they don't want you in one place, go to the other one because those are the ones that really want you. You're going to a first-class place. The organization is first class, the city is great, you're probably going to enjoy it.' He was scared. He was very scared. He kept crying and then his mother wanted to talk to him. He always listened to his mother. He got advice from me, but any time he was upset he talked to his mother."

"I said forget the house, forget everything," Maria says. "That's the past. You go over there, you try to do your best for the people and for the town. You tell me if you still feel sad in two or three months. You need to be there, stay over there with the people. I tell my kids, when something happens like this, it is good. When they trade you, you have to say, that's for the best."

"I had my computer hooked up and I was looking at the press releases going over AP and I saw this story about the trade," Gwynn says. "I couldn't believe it. I tried to call Robbie and his phone was busy. I knew people were calling him because Robbie was loved in San Diego. He was one of those guys who was going to be The Man in San Diego. I said it then, I'll say it now — that was one of the worst trades this organization has ever made. Not only on his part but on Carter's part too. It's hard for me to say that because McGriff is such a great player."

"I was downtown in San Diego somewhere," Jack McKeon remembers of the day the trade was announced. "I had a lunch with somebody, and at about 1:30, I got in my car to drive home. I turned on the radio and I just heard the tail end of the thing — the Padres, Roberto Alomar, Joe Carter to the Toronto Blue Jays. It just sounded to me like it was a rumoured trade. I didn't get that the deal had been completed. Well, I drove a few more miles and they broke in on the station to repeat the bulletin — the Padres have traded Roberto Alomar and Joe Carter to the Blue Jays for Fred McGriff and Tony Fernandez. I said, 'Oh, Jesus Christ.' I almost drove off the road. I said, 'This is crazy, man.' Then I drove back to my house and called Robbie and he was crying. I tried to console him, I told him this might be the greatest thing. You have the opportunity to be a star over there in Toronto. 'Just relax,' I said. 'It's something you can't do anything about, Robbie.' I must have really picked him up, because a few days later his father called me and told me he really appreciated the fact that I called him and tried to encourage him. I'm quite sure today he believes the trade is the greatest thing that ever happened to him.

"He could have been the most popular player that ever played in San Diego. He was the fans' favourite.

He's young. He's got nowhere to go for three more years. He can't become a free agent. I guess Greg Riddoch didn't like him. He fired Sandy Sr., and I guess he figured, 'I'm going to have to live with the kid. The kid's going to be disenchanted all year because his father got fired.' I think he thought like it might be a threat to him, so let's get rid of him.

"Roberto was making two or three hundred thousand dollars a year, tops. You look at the Padres today. When I left them, when they fired me, we were a contending ballclub. We finished fourth that year, but we had an off year. It was a contending ballclub if you left it alone. The manager replaced me, he didn't like Garry Templeton, he wanted to get rid of Templeton. He didn't like Roberto because he fired his old man and figured there was going to be a problem there. Jack Clark and Tony Gwynn were having squabbles, which was no big deal — it was more media than anything. But still he decides we'll get rid of Jack Clark and bring in a first baseman. And then they didn't like Joe Carter because I signed him to a three-year deal and the new owners thought it was going to be too much money. But if you had kept that team together, they would have won the division the next year."

"I could understand them trading me," Joe Carter says. "But not Alomar. He was twenty-two years old, a potential hall of famer. Why would you trade him?"

"You're not going to trade away a young guy like him," Sandy Jr. says. "That was kind of stupid, I thought. That really, really shocked me."

The dust had hardly settled when Roberto got on a plane for his first visit to his new home. There was a card show scheduled for Toronto, where he would do an autograph session. The next day, he would meet

Pat Gillick for the first time, get a look at the stadium, and try to get a feel for the city. Winter had arrived in southern Ontario by the time Alomar landed. A cab took him to the SkyDome Hotel, which is part of the same structure that houses the ballpark. Some of the rooms there face the field. Alomar's faced Front Street. He opened the curtains and tried to understand this frozen foreign land.

"It was snowing. It was cold. I didn't know what to expect. I was in shock. I had seen snow when I played in Reno, but I'd never seen anything like that. I was in the hotel and I could see it snowing through the window. I saw a cop stopping all the cars. It was weird. You couldn't see anybody walking out on the streets. I went there and signed autographs at the show. I was supposed to stay there for two days and I decided not to. I decided to go home. I got a plane ticket for the next day, and I got stuck in the airport for one hour because there was so much snow."

He wouldn't be back until spring. By then he would be more familiar with his teammates, with his new manager, with the American League, with the whole notion of being a Blue Jay. But in his new hometown, Roberto still felt like he had a lot to learn, as well as something to prove.

"I went to Toronto and nobody knew who I was," he says. "Everybody knew Joe Carter — he had played in the American League. Nobody knew who Roberto Alomar was. My dad told me and my mom told me. 'You'd better go there and let them know who you are.' So I went there and I was kind of scared in the beginning, because I didn't know where I was going. I went there and tried to do my best. I started slowly, but after that I started to know a little more about the city, about the people."

7

 BLUE JAY

In the spring of 1991, Roberto Alomar reported to the Toronto Blue Jays' camp in Dunedin, Florida, a quiet town full of retirees on the Gulf Coast just up the road from the resort city of Clearwater. There weren't many familiar faces around the Cecil P. Englebert Recreational Complex. He had met Kelly Gruber and Dave Stieb when he played with a group of major league All Stars who toured Japan in 1990. And of course, his San Diego teammate Joe Carter was arriving at the same time. "I think I'm still closest to him because I came with him," Roberto says. "I can go to him and ask him anything if I have a problem. We don't hang out that much away from the park, because he has a family that he has to take care of. Still I consider him like my brother."

This was a different team, a different league and a different situation. While the Padres seemed to be spinning their wheels, building and rebuilding without ever getting over the top, the Toronto franchise had been run with all but faultless logic. Born in 1977, the Blue

Jays became the model of how to build a contender out of an expansion team as quickly as possible, and then how to keep it at or near the top season after season without ever really cleaning house.

The Jays had suffered the usual trauma associated with starting a team from scratch, losing over one hundred games their first three seasons and ninety-five in their fourth. But in the meantime, the organization assembled a strong farm system, it acquired young talent from other teams through the draft, and it selectively added veterans. By 1983, the Jays' seventh season of existence, Toronto finished sixteen games above .500 and nine games out of first place. Two years later, the club won its first division title, losing the American League Championship Series to the Kansas City Royals — the eventual World Series champions — after being up three games to one.

That loss was disappointing to the rapidly growing number of baseball fans in Toronto, but there was every reason to expect that the Jays would soon have another chance, and that as their young players matured, they would only improve. This was apparently a dynasty in the making.

Instead, what ensued was the franchise's most difficult period since its first years. Jimy Williams, the team's third base coach, was promoted to manager after Bobby Cox left for Atlanta following the 1985 season. His appointment was one of the few out-and-out disasters in the club's administrative history. In 1986, 1987 and 1988, the Blue Jays were always in contention in the American League East, but fell short of winning a second division title. A particularly dramatic collapse in the last week of 1987 earned the team a reputation for gagging when the going got tough. The only way the Jays could shake that "chokers" label would be to go all the way to a championship.

When Toronto got off to a terrible start in 1989, Williams was fired thirty-six games into the season — the first manager axed in mid-season in franchise history. The team's hitting coach, Clarence Edwin (Cito) Gaston, whose playing career had been spent mostly with the San Diego Padres and who had been selected to play in the 1970 All Star Game, was given the managing job on an interim basis — with management indicating strongly that he was not their choice to take over the job full time. Gaston himself seemed indifferent to the prospect, saying that he was perfectly happy in his coaching role, and didn't yet aspire to a managerial job.

Eventually, though, he was confirmed as manager for the remainder of the 1989 season. After their disastrous 12–24 beginning under Williams, the Jays went 77–49 the rest of the way and won their second division title. They advanced to the ALCS, where to no one's surprise they were no match for the powerful American League West champions, the Oakland Athletics, losing in five games.

In 1990, despite a late charge, the Jays fell just short of Boston in the American League East. That failure prompted the shake-up that included the trade that brought Alomar to Toronto. By making such significant changes, the Jays were acknowledging that the group of players that had come of age together in the 1980s was never going to be good enough to win a World Series. Instead, they would go in a new direction, with Alomar, Carter and Devon White, a brilliant defensive centrefielder who had been acquired by Gillick in a trade with the California Angels.

Alomar and Carter were pretty much known quantities, but White was a bit of a reclamation project. He had enormous skills, but he had become discouraged in California when he came under attack in the press as the quality of his play fell off.

"I've known Devon for a long time," Roberto says. "He was criticized a lot in California. People said he wasn't giving his maximum. He was giving the maximum; he was giving his best. But they criticized him so early in his career that maybe he put a lot of pressure on himself. They traded him, and when he came to Toronto, he said all I have to do is look forward, go to another team and do my best. He did a great job and proved those guys wrong. He quieted a lot of people. They had to stick their tongues inside their mouths."

Those three newcomers arrived at spring training in 1991 not necessarily as saviours, but certainly accompanied by some sky-high fan expectations. They had been acquired at a high price for one reason and one reason only: to lead Toronto to a world championship. "I went to spring training, and people started seeing who I was. They were looking at me and Joe," Alomar says. "Everybody knew who Joe was but nobody knew who Roberto Alomar was. They didn't see me that much when I was playing for San Diego. I was kind of shaky, but I went out there and did my job. I got used to the players and got used to the management. I made a good relationship with my teammates. That's real important."

One of the first people in the Toronto organization that Roberto got to know was his new manager, though it wouldn't be until the regular season that he really began to understand how Cito Gaston handled his job.

Coming off his souring experience with Greg Riddoch in San Diego, it was important that he establish a good working relationship with the man who would lead his new club. They bonded quickly, and for good reason. Roberto wanted to be treated with respect, to be allowed to play the game, to be trusted — and in return he would be a team man all the way. Gaston wanted to treat his players as he would have wanted to be treated when he played. He wasn't a screamer, he didn't play head games, he wouldn't impose unreasonable discipline. His ideal player was a grown-up who accepted responsibility and who worked at both playing and understanding the game. He and Roberto fit like hand and glove.

"Before the trade, I hadn't really seen Robbie play, but I knew Joe Carter. Joe said to me, 'You're going to like this kid. He can really play the game,'" Cito Gaston says. "The first thing I noticed about Robbie that spring is that he loves to play. He has fun playing baseball. And he has great instincts for the game, on defence or on offence. He knows the play that he wants to make before it happens. For a young kid, he's really years ahead of a lot of people. He's a student of the game. I don't think it hurts that he comes from a baseball background. He doesn't really need to be coached much. He's just gifted with a lot of talent, plus he's a hard worker."

"Cito's an easy-going guy," Alomar says. "He's the kind of manager that just lets you play the game. He's good to have on your side because he's a player's manager. People think that he's not real aggressive. All he tells you is to go out there and give one hundred percent or you'll be on the bench. That's the way to do it because we're not kids. We know what to do. Suppose you're thirty years old. You have a family to take care of just like he has a family to take care of. You respect him and he respects you. But if you do something out of line, he will tell you. I remember one time when David Wells did something to him and he went and talked to him, and after that everything was okay.

"Cito's just a great person. You cannot say anything bad about him. Whenever he has something to say to you, he says it to your face. He doesn't show you up. He says, 'let's go talk in the office.' You talk man to man. He will not stab you in the back, none of that. He's a gentleman and everyone respects him. The press doesn't understand what is inside the club-house, because this is a family. We cannot tell every-thing to the press. And Cito will not go out there to the press and talk about his players. That's why the press doesn't like him, and that's why the players respect him. Because whatever we say on the inside, it stays on the inside.

"A lot of people say he's too soft on his players. He's not soft. When he has to say something, he'll say it to you. People say he's not doing a good job, but three times he has been in the championship series. I never have conflicts with him because I do my job. And as long as I do my job I will have no problems with him. He gives me some tips whenever I'm slumping. He'll say, 'Roberto, you're doing this wrong.' Whenever I'm in trouble, he'll say, 'Roberto, do you have a problem?' and we'll talk as men, as friends. He doesn't say that much. He just lets you play the game. He doesn't put pressure on his players. They just understand their job.

"Some people think that he's too loyal to his players. Whenever he has to be tough, he can be tough. Maybe sometimes some of the guys take advantage of him. I will not say any names — there are always a few who will try to do that. But really, you couldn't. He's a real smart man."

Spring training is a relaxing ritual for ballplayers, at least when they're not life-and-death to win a spot on the opening day roster. "It's a good time," Roberto says, "a time to get to know your teammates, to talk to them and have a good relationship. It's a time when you can go out and work for the perfection of your game. What you were doing wrong last year you want to do right this year. If you want to run more, if you want to steal more bases, you have to work on it. If you want to be a better infielder, you can work on that. You can talk to different players and get different ideas about what we can do to win. So many things get done in spring training."

When he was with the Padres, springs were spent in Yuma, Arizona, a town in the southwest corner of the state near the Mexican border. There, the players stayed together in the same hotel, and stuck together away from the ballpark, since there wasn't a whole lot else to do. "You can see the other players in the pool with their wives and their kids," Roberto says. "You spend a lot of time with the other players." Local fans came to the park, and San Diego fans trekked across the desert for Cactus League games. But still, it seemed far from the spotlight.

Dunedin was a different matter. The Blue Jays had exploded in popularity across Canada, setting a major league attendance record in 1990, and enough Canadians spent their winter vacations in Florida to make tickets to even exhibition games extremely scarce. "It was totally different than in Yuma," Roberto says. "There were a lot of fans, a lot of media. It was a different atmosphere."

Hopes were soaring by the time the team came north to begin the regular season, Roberto moved into a room in the SkyDome Hotel — the same place he had stayed on his first, abortive visit to the city the previous winter. Since the team moved into the SkyDome, many Blue Jay players have made the hotel a temporary home. Because it is actually part of the same building that houses the stadium, it is the most convenient location possible. They can go from their room to the clubhouse without ever setting foot outdoors.

But usually, after a short period of time, the players move elsewhere. Those who are single, or who are married without children, often make their home in one of the chic condominiums that line the city's lakefront. Others, with children, sometimes move to the suburbs. Roberto, though, moved to the hotel and stayed in the hotel for his first season, his second season, and he plans to be there for his third. He rents an apartment in San Juan and another in Florida near the Jays' spring training home, but in Toronto he sees no reason to live anywhere else.

"A lot of people ask me why I live in the hotel?" he says. "But if they could see it, and if they knew how they treated me there, they would understand. It's great. I'm single. I have a big room. I have everything. I have two TVs. I have a VCR. I have drawers for my clothing. I have laundry service. A maid comes to clean my room every day. I have a radio. I have everything that you can have in an apartment. The only thing I don't have is a kitchen, and I'm not going to cook anyway. Not when I can call room service any time."

It wasn't just the hotel's amenities that made Roberto's life there so appealing. As it turned out, the room came not just with a view, but also with a surro-gate mom.

Betty John is nobody's fool. She is a strong, formi-dable woman who looks people straight in the eye and says what she thinks, who gives the impression of someone not easily swayed. In the winter of 1991, while working as the SkyDome Hotel's communica-tions supervisor, she received a call about a guest who was about to check into the hotel, a young man who would become a big part of her job, and a big part of her life.

"A very good friend of mine who is also a very good friend of the Alomar family asked me to keep an eye on Robbie, because here was a young guy, coming to Toronto and not knowing anyone," she remembers. "He said because you work here and because he's going to be staying here, just keep an eye on him. I called Robbie on the phone and said, 'my name is Betty John.' He said, 'oh yeah, I heard about you.' It started out as me doing a favour for a friend, but as time went by that friend went out the window and Robbie and I developed our own relationship. Robbie is 24 — my eldest son is 33. So we developed a sort of mother-son relationship. We became friends. I found that I could talk to him, I could trust him. I could tell him things and I knew that I wasn't going to hear it outside."

Roberto obviously feels the same way. Seeing him, day in and day out during the baseball season, in good times and bad, Betty John has a special understanding of his personality. While others see the player on the field, she sees a young man finding his way in the world. At the hotel, she screens his calls, helps him deal with mail, makes sure that he isn't disturbed. And when he needs someone to talk to, she — like his mother — is the one Roberto turns to.

"He's so spoiled around here, it ain't funny," Betty John says. "This is his home and we're his family. From the doorman to the room attendant, we all know him. He walks in here and it's like he's coming home to his family. We all protect him in here and we all do whatever we can to make him happy. If he's hungry, he calls room service. He gets his room cleaned every day. What more can a man ask for?

"The Robbie that I have seen is one that a lot of people will never see because they do not deal with him every day the way I do. Robbie's got to be one of the kindest people that you'll ever get to meet. A guy who would really give you the shirt off his back. He likes people and he wants people to like him in return. He was brought up — he wasn't dragged up by his parents. He believes in God — firmly believes in God — and that has come from the teachings of his parents. If you notice Robbie before he bats, he always makes the sign of the Cross. He's really, really warm hearted. He is shy — make no two ways about that. Robbie is very, very shy. He sits there and he won't say anything. He'll be signing autographs and his head is down. He'll look up and see something but then his head goes back down. But once he gets to know you, you can't get the guy to shut up. It's yap, yap, yap, yap. He's no dummy. He's no fool. You can't fool him. You can't pull the wool over his eyes. Even if he thinks you're not genuine, he will still be genuine with you. That's the kind of person he is.

"He's not the kind of kid that could come up to you and say, 'I love you.' You're not going to hear that. But he's the type of kid that's going to do something so out of the blue to let you know the way he feels about you.

And he has a very playful side. He likes to sing; he likes to dance. You should see him doing all these dances in his room, dancing all over the place and singing. You have to sit and listen to him sing Spanish songs. I said to him, I'm very happy you have another profession. This is the childish side of Robbie that people out there don't see. Him taking a pillow and throwing it at you, or you're passing him and he'll tug your hair or pinch you or tickle you or something like that. When he does that, you know this kid is okay today. There's lots of adrenaline flowing. It figures that Robbie loves kids. You should see him with them — it's absolutely priceless. He's not shy with kids. With kids, he is a kid. He'll make a terrific father. I don't know what he's waiting on. He'd better hurry, or I'll be too old to change diapers.

"His success hasn't changed him. I hope he never gets to be swell-headed. So far here's a kid with all these millions, and up to now he's not a little snot. His money has not gone to his head, and I hope it never does. Knowing the kind of family he is from, I don't think they would permit him to get like that. If he ever let his success go to his head, Sandy Alomar Sr. would be right there to bring him down."

The Blue Jays began the 1991 season better than any other team in the history of the franchise, winning six of their first eight games. But after that, they faltered, finishing the first month of the season in fourth place, with an unremarkable record of 12–10. Like his teammates, Roberto didn't really find his form in April either. He hit .256 and drove in just six runs.

On May 1, the Jays played the Texas Rangers, with Nolan Ryan — Roberto's childhood tutor, and the pitcher in his first major league at-bat — on the mound.

Alomar would be Ryan's sixteenth strikeout victim that night, and the final out of his seventh career no-hitter. "I remember Roberto Alomar as a little toddler running around our clubhouse," Ryan said after the game. "I guess that says something about how old I am that I'm pitching to the sons of former teammates."

"You've got to admire him," Roberto says. "Not too many people can do what he's been doing. You don't feel happy to strike out against him, but you feel happy because you're in history now. Every time they talk about his seventh no-hitter, they have to talk about me."

For Roberto and the ballclub, that brush with history signalled a new beginning. The Blue Jays hit their stride, climbing into first place by June 3. Alomar had one of the greatest months of his career. He hit five home runs in May, including one from each side of the plate against Chicago on May 10, becoming the fifty-fifth player in major league history to accomplish the feat. He also had six doubles, three triples and drove in nineteen runs, giving the fans in Toronto their first taste of the true impact of the big trade.

"I didn't know the pitchers that much," Roberto says. "I was learning about the league. After that I started hitting pretty good, I started knowing the people much better, I started stealing more bases."

Something else that happened to Toronto that month would have major repercussions for the rest of the season. Dave Stieb, long the ace of the Toronto starting staff, collided with a runner while covering first and hurt his back. While the injury would be diagnosed as relatively minor at first, it would in fact end Stieb's season, and he would never again be an effective pitcher in a Blue Jay uniform. Desperately searching for a replacement, Toronto called up a young pitcher originally from the Dominican Republic who had been playing for their Syracuse AAA farm team, where he had an unspectacular 4–5 record with a 4.03 ERA. But Juan Guzman, who the Jays had picked up in a trade with the Los Angeles Dodgers in 1987, would make those and all of his other minor league statistics look irrelevant by the time the season was done. A year later, he would be the best pitcher on the best team in baseball.

"I saw Guzman pitch in the bullpen in spring training," Roberto says. "I didn't know who he was, because I didn't really know the guys there. I asked who this guy throwing hard is. I could see that he had a good arm. He's a good guy, a quiet guy. He works hard. He wasn't intimidated by the big leagues. You cannot be intimidated by coming up. You have to go out there and let your abilities speak for you, and do the job. You know you're going to have some butterflies at the beginning, you're going to be scared. You have to just put your heart there and do your best.

"I talked to him, and he knew that this is what he had been working for. He was real young, but I think the Latin guys get to the big leagues quicker because they start in the minors so young. They cannot go to bars, they cannot go to a lot of places that the American players can go because they aren't over twenty-one. They're thinking about baseball instead of going out partying. They're not staying out late. They have a lot of fun in college. When I was seventeen or eighteen, I couldn't go to bars. So I was thinking more about my job. I was thinking all the time about baseball."

Pat Gillick, acting like someone who saw a championship on the horizon, acquired knuckleballer Tom Candiotti from the Cleveland Indians in return for outfielders Glenallen Hill and Mark Whiten, and pitcher

Denis Boucher. By the All Star break, Toronto led the division by five and a half games, and most of their fans were already talking confidently about the playoffs, and about how this year, it would be different.

The 1991 All Star Game was held in the SkyDome. For the first time, Roberto was selected by the fans as the starting second baseman — this time, of course, for the American League. Sandy was again voted the starting catcher, making the Alomars the first brothers selected to the team since the fans were given the vote in 1970.

It was a wildly emotional moment for the whole family when Sandy and Roberto stood together during the player introductions. The Toronto fans had given their hometown hero the loudest, longest ovations of the evening. Though those in the stands couldn't see it, Roberto began to cry.

"I never thought they were going to give me that ovation," Roberto says. "That's when I started realizing how much they enjoyed seeing me play in Toronto. I felt real good. It was an emotional moment. It was like the people were telling you, 'thank you, thank you for your work, thank you for playing hard.'"

"He was getting sentimental," Sandy Jr. says. "I said Robbie, take it easy, don't cry on national TV. But it's like a dream. It's something you never expect to accomplish. You go back in your childhood when you were playing in the Little League, and now here you are, in the best baseball league in the world, playing in the All Star Game. It's a feeling you can't describe."

"Seeing all those people give Robbie that ovation was a great experience," Sandy Sr. says. "He was crying and Sandy had to hug him. Seeing them next to each other, and hearing that ovation, hearing the cheers come down and Sandy hugging him. That was wonderful."

After the All Star break, the Blue Jays continued their torrid pace, stretching their division lead to eight games over the surprising Detroit Tigers, who despite an extremely thin pitching staff were having a great season under Sparky Anderson. It looked like Toronto would cakewalk to the pennant until they hit the skids in August, losing seven games in a row. It didn't help that their manager was trying to keep his mind in the game while suffering through excruciating back pain. Gaston's sciatica finally forced him into the hospital on August 21, with Gene Tenace, the team's hitting instructor, taking over the field manager's duties. Gaston wouldn't be able to return to the dugout until September 27.

The Tigers continued to close the gap, and finally pulled into a first-place tie with Toronto on August 24. All of the cynics in the crowd were suggesting that despite the new cast, these were really the same old Blow Jays — except this was worse. Here they were on the verge of losing the division to a team that, on paper, wasn't nearly their equal.

The new Jays silenced their critics fast. Led by Alomar, who had a torrid September and October — hitting .322, and driving in 12 runs — the Jays buried the Tigers, and then held off a late charge by the Boston Red Sox. The division championship was theirs, the second in three years, the third in franchise history. Alomar finished the season with career highs in hits (188), RBIs (69), stolen bases (53) and runs scored (88) — the last number in no small part a tribute to Carter, who drove in 108 runs, the fifth time in six seasons that he had recorded more than 100 RBIs. Roberto also tied his career best batting average, .295, and his career high in home runs, with nine. He was named the Blue Jays' player of the month for May, July and September, and at the end of the year was named the team's most valuable player by the local chapter of the Baseball Writers of America.

Combined with the fact that White put up some of the best numbers of his career, the three players who had arrived the previous winter had made Gillick look like a genius. Now, though, came the part that really counted. Other Blue Jay clubs had gone this far. This one was supposed to take the next step.

It would be their first experience in the post-season for Alomar, Carter and White, and after years playing for also-rans, they were more than happy to be there. But for those who had experienced the crushing loss to Oakland in 1989, or the heartbreak against Kansas City in 1985, the situation was a little bit more loaded. This would be their chance to atone, to shake the choke label once and for all.

"In 1991, three-quarters of the team had already been in the playoffs and lost, so they were only looking at the World Series," Joe Carter says. "The rest of us, though — Robbie and Devo and I — we felt like we had a great season just getting to the playoffs. We'd never been there before."

"It meant a lot to me. I'd never been to the playoffs before. The people were there, they made a lot of noise," Alomar says. "People outside were watching TV all over the world. It's something that you work for. Joe and I had never been there before, so it was different for us."

There was every reason to suspect that Toronto would finally make it as far as the World Series. Minnesota wasn't considered a powerhouse like the 1989

Oakland team had been. The Jays had played four series against the Twins during the regular season, and won each of them two games to one. Minnesota hit just .218 off Toronto pitching, with only 21 extra base hits. And the home field advantage — even in the raucous Metrodome — didn't appear to be much of a factor. Over the past two seasons, the Blue Jays had won ten of the twelve games played there, and so when they set off for Minneapolis to play games one and two, there was no shortage of confidence.

Some were surprised that the knuckleballer, Candiotti, was given the all-important start in the opening game of the series — especially since Guzman had been all but unhittable in the second half of the season, at one point winning ten starts in a row. But Candiotti had handled the Twins well in the past, and Alomar, at least, wasn't going to do any second guessing of those above him in the Blue Jay hierarchy.

"You have to be behind that kind of decision," he says. "Whatever they say, you have to follow."

After game one, a lot other people would not be so willing to follow, though. Candiotti's knuckler wasn't dancing, and his other pitches looked like batting practice fodder to the Twins' hitters. Before the third inning was done, the Jays were already into their bullpen, and were down five runs. They rallied back against Minnesota starter Jack Morris, pulling to within a run in the sixth inning, but that's the way it would finish: 5–4 Twins.

For Morris, whose career had appeared on the wane when he lost eighteen games for Detroit in 1990, it was the beginning of a remarkable playoff. He would get stronger and stronger as the post-season went on, winning two games in the ALCS and two games in the

World Series, including one of the most courageous big-game performances of all time, a ten-inning shutout against Atlanta in the seventh and deciding game to win the world championship.

When the post-mortems were done on the 1991 Blue Jays and why they weren't quite good enough, the missing ingredient usually cited was "a guy like Jack Morris" — a gutsy, ferocious competitor, a winner who wouldn't be denied.

"Morris was tough," Roberto says. "I was hitting real good. We handled him okay. We scored runs on him but they scored back. And Jack is the kind of guy that all you have to do is keep him in the game and he will win in the end. You just have to stay in the game, and he's sort of like a horse. He'll never quit. He goes out there and pitches until his arm falls off. He's not scared to pitch. He pitches with the score. He's not afraid to throw strikes, he's not afraid to throw his fastball when he gets behind."

The second game of the ALCS seemed to shift momentum Toronto's way. Guzman was given the start, and he showed no sign of rookie nerves, giving up two runs in 5.2 innings, while the Jays scored three runs early to take the lead. Tom Henke was first out of the bullpen, followed by Duane Ward, and the Twins could do no more damage, while the Jays added two insurance runs to win 5–2. They returned home for three games at the SkyDome knowing that the home field advantage was now theirs, and the World Series was closer than it had been since 1985.

In game three, the Jays jumped out to an early 2–0 lead on a Joe Carter home run and a Candy Maldonado RBI double. Then, in the fifth inning, chasing a ball to the rightfield fence, Carter injured his ankle. He would stay in the game and take his turn at the plate in the seventh inning, but he wasn't the same and he wouldn't be the same for the remainder of the series. The Jays would go on to lose the game in extra innings on Mike Pagliarulo's home run, but Carter's injury was still the most significant blow of the night, one from which Toronto would never really recover.

"Joe never played for a club that was a contender," Pat Gillick said, paying tribute to Carter's courage in trying to continue to play. "Some players are very comfortable with a sixth or seventh place club. Sometimes guys don't react to a change like that. But Joe did."

"That hurt us a lot because Joe wasn't the same," Roberto says. "He was playing but he couldn't run, and he wasn't swinging the bat the way he usually does. That's when you saw what he really meant to the club. When he got hurt and he could not play rightfield and he could not give that much. Still in his heart he wanted to play, but he wasn't one hundred percent. He couldn't do what he wanted to. But he knew that if he took himself out of the lineup it would be worse. When you're missing one of your big guys, it's always tough. The team is not the same. It's like you're missing a piece, and you must have all the pieces together to feel comfortable."

With Minnesota now up two games to one, the Jays knew that the best they could hope for was to send the series back to Minnesota. And they knew they would have to do it with their best run producer severely hobbled. The team responded with two of the most dispiriting losses in the history of the franchise.

Going with a four-man rotation, Cito Gaston sent Todd Stottlemyre against Morris in game four. The Jays were down 4-1 after four, finally lost 9-3, as Morris pitched eight strong innings for Minnesota, allowing just two runs. In game five, the Jays looked like they were going to at least go down fighting, running up an early 5-2 lead before blowing it in the late innings.

The final score was 8–5 Minnesota. The Blue Jays had fallen short again.

"We didn't hit much with men on base," Roberto says, summing up the series. "We weren't getting a lot of production from the bottom part of the lineup. We made a few mistakes; we didn't run the bases well. Sometimes the pitching struggled a bit. It was a little bit of everything."

Alomar, though, played an exceptional series, hitting .474 to lead the team, driving in four runs, stealing two bases. His first playoff experience had been an unqualified personal success — but afterwards, those statistics didn't mean much. The team had failed to reach its goals, and Roberto took the loss hard.

"I was disappointed, that's for sure," he says. "But we did our best. I wanted to go all the way to the World Series and I felt like we had the team to do it. But if it is not meant to be, it is not meant to be. I just went home and watched the World Series on television. I was glad with the job that I did. But they played better baseball than us."

At the time, though, at least in private, he wasn't quite so philosophical about what had happened.

"Last year when they lost in the playoffs, I've never seen Robbie that sad," Betty John remembers. "He wanted to win so bad he could taste it. When he gets down he's very, very quiet. He'll go off in a corner. It bothers him. It really bothers him. He can get down harder on himself than I think Cito Gaston or anyone else can."

8

 A STAR IS BORN

During his life in and around baseball, in the United
States and Puerto Rico, Roberto Alomar had learned
something about the aura of celebrity that surrounds
those who play the game for a living. But nothing in his
experience prepared him for what his life would be like
as a marquee player for the Toronto Blue Jays in the
early 1990s.

Twenty-five years before, when his father was first in
the big leagues, public interest in the private lives of
ballplayers wasn't nearly so intense. Baseball itself was
in a period of decline, in the process of being eclipsed
by professional football as the most television-friendly
sport in North America. Sandy Sr., who was a utility
player for most of his career, was never really a star,
unlike some of those he played beside, and unlike
even a couple of his managers. Only in Puerto Rico
was Sandy a household name, and a celebrity. Such
was his fame that you can still see his image, wearing
a Yankee uniform, as part of a mural on the wall

surrounding the baseball stadium in Salinas, the Alomars' hometown.

There is a big, big difference, though, between being the most famous ballplayer in a little town on the southern coast of Puerto Rico, and being the most popular baseball player in Toronto in the last decade of this century. Since the beginnings of the Blue Jay franchise, the sport had been a major commercial success in southern Ontario, and to a degree all across Canada. Some savvy marketing in the early days, when the product on the field left something to be desired, built a core following who turned out in decent numbers despite the less-than-comfortable surroundings of Exhibition Stadium. But in those early years, baseball existed in balance with the other professional sports in town: hockey and football. The Maple Leafs of the National Hockey League were still closest to the hearts of local sports enthusiasts, at least those old enough to remember their glory years of the 1960s. Through the late 1970s, the Argonauts of the Canadian Football League drew large, enthusiastic crowds through the summer and fall.

From 1985 on, though, as the Jays emerged as one of the best and most exciting teams in baseball, interest in the game skyrocketed, and the balance among sports in Toronto shifted. The Leafs' sad seasons under the ownership of Harold Ballard, and the Argos' passivity in marketing and fall from fashionable status helped to open the door (although the latter may have been in part a byproduct of the Blue Jays' ascendance), and the Jays stepped in. By the time the SkyDome opened in 1989, the Jays were on an entirely different plane from the other teams, in many ways the only game in town. Everyone, it seemed, was a baseball fan. Everyone was in front of a television or tuned in on radio during a pennant race. In 1991, Roberto's first year with the club, the Blue Jays drew a major league record 4,001,526 fans, and that number was a real reflection of what had become a mania.

There were plenty of baseball fans in San Diego too, of course, where Roberto had begun his major league career and earned his first accolades. But there the spotlight was already divided up among established stars, first among them the great hitter Tony Gwynn, and there the team had been through enough ups and (especially) downs that the population was a bit jaded, the way most fans of most teams are a bit jaded.

Not Torontonians, though, at least not about baseball. Their heroes were treated to enormous affection, even the relative newcomers. For Roberto Alomar, it had begun with the extra attention in spring training; it had built as he found his stride in May; it had welled up with the emotional ovation at the All Star Game; and it had reached new heights through the stretch drive and the playoffs. He would head home to Puerto Rico for the winter, but there would be frequent trips north for public appearances, and, of course, there was the season ahead living in the SkyDome Hotel. The first time he'd come there, he had felt alone and unknown in the city. Now, it seemed like the whole town wanted to know everything about him.

"Sometimes it's best to leave an organization to really grow," Tony Gwynn says. "Once Robbie left San Diego, he became the player that everyone knew he could be. He didn't have anything to deal with besides playing baseball. Whereas here, they talked about his dad and they tried to move him to short. People thought he was lackadaisical. Now, seeing him in Toronto, he's just a complete player. He does everything well. He's The Man, and he's earned everything he's got. He won't tell you this, but he likes being in that situation. He likes being The Man. That's one of the things that drives him — to be looked upon as being one of the best."

Roberto, even though he is shy by nature, did enjoy the situation, and didn't shy away from the public interest. He knew that it was all part of the equation.

"It's very important for players — especially Latin players — to associate with the people," he says. "That's a problem we have because we're afraid of the language. But I wasn't that way. I was brought up partly in another culture. I go out and talk to people. There are going to be some good talks and some negative talks, but I don't mind. People have got to know what kind of person you are, know what you like and don't like. If you don't talk to people, they're not going to know you. You have to understand that the fans are the ones that go out and pay to see you play. They want to know who you are, where you come from, all that sort of thing.

"I don't hide from anybody because I don't have to hide. I'm a single man. I like to have fun — the right way. I don't go to bars and get drunk. I'm a real low-key guy. I just like to have fun with people. If I see someone who is going to embarrass me, I don't say anything to that person. I just walk away. I don't have to fight with the guy. I've got to let them know that I respect them so they respect me. You're a public guy. You don't want people talking about you.

"Of course, when you're in the public eye, there is going to be a lot of jealousy. I hear a few comments in Toronto that I'm this way, or I'm that. Sometimes people get the wrong idea about you. Some people have the idea that I'm cocky on the field. That I show

off. Really, I always was a quiet guy. I don't like to show
people up. I just like the game. When I play the game,
it's a fun game. I like to have fun. That's what some
people don't understand. Cocky can be different
things. It can be a guy who goes out there and shows
everybody up. Or cocky can be a guy going out there
and having fun — the right way — and not showing
anybody up. But when I hear things, it really doesn't
bug me. The people that are saying that are jealous. My
mom and dad told me that if people talk about you, it
means they like you. Don't worry about it. Whenever
they don't talk about you, that's when you have to worry
about it.

"I have my friends. I know who to trust and who not
to trust. My best friends are my mom and my dad, my
brother and my sister. Those are my best friends, all in
the family. And Christie, my sister-in-law, I really trust
her. She really helped me a lot. She helped my brother
a lot. She's one of the nicest persons I've met outside
of my family. For me, there are only a few people I can
trust. You make all of this money and you don't know
what people are here for. Are they there for the money
or are they there because they like you?"

As fans began to realize that Roberto lived in the
hotel — and since the hotel was right next to the park,
and in many ways a public space — there were frequent
occasions when they would hang out in the lobby
waiting for him, or try to find his room, defying the best
efforts of the hotel staff to protect his privacy. Sometimes his phone calls are intercepted, sometimes they
go right through to his room. "Fans call him and he
answers the phone," says Betty John. "He doesn't hide
from his fans. There are a lot of kids who call, and he
talks to them."

Along with kids, much of the attention Roberto receives is from young women. As a single man, he has become something of a sex symbol on the local sporting scene. With that reputation goes a lot of talk that he lives the kind of wild social life that has been associated with some professional athletes.

"A lot of people think that Robbie likes to party, party, party. I have heard a lot of people talk about how Robbie is out partying every night and getting down and boogying. That's a misconception because it just isn't him," says Betty John. "Robbie likes home, home, home. Robbie is quite happy renting five or six videos and sitting down and watching them. He'd rather do that than go out to some club. Many of the times, you will see him watching old baseball tapes. People think that he's got babes lined up around the corner. That's another misconception. He says that he doesn't want to be responsible for hurting anybody. For most young men in his position, the women are lining up, and the guy couldn't care less about the girl's reputation or what people think or anything like that. He's the complete opposite. Part of it is he's thinking about his own reputation."

"Robbie likes to go out with girls, because this is the time for him," his mother, Maria, says. "But I tell him to be careful. Sometimes he's lonely. He needs his family. Sometimes he calls me and says, Mom, come over here."

Of course, Roberto does meet women and he does go out to the city's clubs and restaurants. But in a lot of ways, he says, his life is no different from anyone else's, except that his celebrity status has actually made it more difficult to strike up real relationships.

"It's complicated," he says. "When you're in the public eye and you go out with a girl, everybody thinks you're sleeping with the girl. It's not that way. I've got to have some female friends and I've got to have some male friends. I want people to understand that I'm a human being. The way life is going now, you have to be careful about who you go out with. I have friends, but I want people to understand that when I go out with a girl or a guy, I'm not doing something wrong. I get real mad sometimes because people don't know, and they talk a little bit too much. I can be a sportsman. I can be in the public eye. But not everybody's the same. You have to know me as a person. I never in my life have used drugs. I'm not an alcoholic — I maybe go out for one drink or two drinks, but you will never see me drunk. I'm only twenty-four, but I know what's going on in life. I want people to know that I'm not stupid. I know what I'm doing. All I'm concerned with is to treat people nice. The nicer I treat people, the nicer they are going to treat me.

"The bottom line is that I'm a fun guy to be with. I'm like a normal guy. It's kind of tough to go out right now, but I like to go out to clubs and dance. I like to go out and eat — I like Centro, Splendido. For fun I go to the Loose Moose, or Alice Fazoolis, Stilife, Paparazzi, Jaguar. I go to a lot of places. I like to go to the movies. I like to play miniature golf. And I like to stay home. I'm not a real wild guy. I've been raised pretty good. When the team is on the road, I usually just hang around by myself. Sometimes if I see Joe around, or Manuel Lee or Devon White, or Alfredo, or Candy, I'll go out and eat with them. After the game on road trips, I usually just go back to my room. In Texas, I used to go to Ruben Sierra's house to eat, and in Cleveland, I go to my brother's house. But that's about it. I know some players have fun in the bars on the road, but I don't know if they bring it back up to their rooms. That's none of my business. I take care of myself. I don't know what they do.

"My mom told me that somebody's your girlfriend when she has your ring on her finger. There's no one like that for me right now. It's tough. Women sometimes look for love, sometimes they look for money, sometimes they just want to take advantage of you. Those are three different things right there. You, as a man, what are you going to do? You don't know what to do. You don't know what they are here for. If a girl goes to a guy who is nobody, who doesn't have a name — maybe he's a big lawyer, but nobody knows he's a big lawyer — and goes out with that guy, are they going to say anything about that guy? But if a girl says, 'I was going out with Roberto Alomar,' people say, 'Oh yeah, the second baseman for the Toronto Blue Jays.' It's a big deal. Remember when they put in the papers what happened with Wade Boggs? That's the kind of thing I'm real mad about. Why are we different than the other people?

"I know I'm not going to settle down with one person for a while. At this stage, I cannot be tied to one person. I cannot be married. I'm too young. And it's tough to know if these girls are here for me or for the money. I want to take care of my business first. I want to have what I want to have. I want to make what I want to make. I want to make sure that whatever I have now, it's going to be mine forever. I don't want to get married and get divorced and just break a relationship like that and break up my family. For me, it's real important that when I get married, I stay married. There's a lot of problems with divorce. I don't want to be in a relationship where, after I earn all this money, the girl is going to come to me and take my money away from me in a divorce. Money's not the only issue, but it's one of the things you think about. You have to be real, real careful with what you do.

"If you're a baseball player, you have to marry a person who understands your job, who understands this game. She has to understand that you're not going to be there all the time, that you're not going to be with your kids all the time. She cannot be with you all the time. But before we have kids, I would want her with me as much as possible. I want to spend time with her. I know my Mom and Dad went through a lot of tough times. I don't want to do the same.

"Those are the kinds of things that you have to think about before you get married. Before I get married, I want to have my own house, my own cars. I want to be okay economically. I want to be able to take care of my kids. I don't want to bring a child into the world like a lot of people do, and leave it in the streets. I want to take care of my child real good. I want my kid to have what I had. I didn't have any problems when I was a kid. I had a roof over my head, I had my bed, I had my food, my private school. My dad had his car. I didn't have to ask for anything. And I had love from my parents. I would like my wife to be home with the kids, the way my mom was, but it's going to be her decision. I wouldn't like to leave my kids with a nanny all the time."

"Robbie doesn't want to marry right now," his mother says. "He doesn't want anything now but baseball. When he's married, he'll have other responsibilities, and he'll have other things on his mind besides baseball. He wants baseball now. He has goals in his head. He wants those before he has other responsibilities."

9

DIFFERENT CAST, DIFFERENT STORY

Maria's other son approached the whole issue of love and marriage very differently.

"I met Christie in 1986 when I was in Beaumont, Texas, in AA," Sandy Jr. says. "She was at the ballpark, she asked for my autograph and I asked her out. That's quick, huh? I asked her if she was doing something after the game. She said no, and that she would give me a ride to get something to eat, and we kept seeing each other. Then she went to Phoenix to work for the IRS. It was kind of hard for us to see each other. But in 1988, I went to AAA, to Las Vegas in the Pacific Coast League. I went to Phoenix and she used to fly to Las Vegas all the time.

"We decided to get married in one of those chapel houses. We talked about it for a few days. My Mom and Dad couldn't come over anyway. They weren't going to do it for a quick wedding — you know how it is in Las Vegas. I just wanted to get married, it wasn't a big deal, just something small. And that was it.

"Sandy called me one hour before he got married," Maria says. "'Mommy?' he said on the phone. I said, 'Sandy, how are you?' He said, 'Mommy, I'm going to get married. I'm waiting in the limousine right now.' I was surprised. But that's Sandy. When Sandy wants something. . . ."

"When he called me, I asked him if he knew what he was doing. It's not easy. Think it over before you do it," Sandy Sr. says. "But at least he had known her for two years."

"I guess I just got attached early," Sandy Jr. says. "I felt like I became a better baseball player after I settled down a little bit and I was married. If I wasn't married, I don't know if I would have even got to the big leagues. Sometimes when you're single, you get a little crazy, you get out of hand. I can't regret that I got married a little early."

Toronto's disappointment in the 1991 American League Championship Series did nothing to cool the fans' ardour for the team, or for Roberto. But as winter approached, there were enough troubling questions about the team's future to dominate many a conversation during the off-season. First was the question of the pitching staff: Dave Stieb had never really recovered from his back problems, and because of the nature of the injury, there was some question whether he would ever be the same. On December 4, 1991, he underwent back surgery, which made the status of the team's long-time ace even more of a question mark for 1992. At the same time, Tom Candiotti, whose acquisition had helped push Toronto over the top, was eligible for free agency, and it soon became clear that he wasn't going to be coming back to the team.

That left Toronto with Jimmy Key, Todd Stottlemyre, David Wells — who had been back and forth between starting and the bullpen — and the rookie phenom Juan Guzman as its starting rotation. That probably wasn't going to be enough to push Toronto to the next level, which for the franchise had become the only level that counted.

The team also needed some more run production. With White and Alomar, there was plenty of speed at the top of the batting order, and Carter could be counted on to drive in another hundred runs. Candy Maldonado, picked up from Milwaukee on waivers in August, had been a good addition, and John Olerud, now at home at first base, had enormous potential. But Kelly Gruber's production had dropped precipitously, in part because of injuries, and none of the designated hitters the team had used — Rance Mulliniks, Dave Parker, Pat Tabler — had really done the job.

Vice president Pat Gillick and president Paul Beeston had plenty of people reminding him that the team still seemed to lack the necessary intangibles to win a championship. The new additions were fine on and off the field, and Guzman was a tenacious competitor who was unaffected by big league pressures, but still the Jays lacked something in the character department. Perhaps they didn't have enough players with the necessary will to win, perhaps the mix of leaders and followers wasn't quite right. Perhaps they just needed a little bit more heart.

That would change when, over two days in December, Beeston took some of the cash that had been pouring into the SkyDome and performed a transplant. On December 18, the Blue Jays signed Jack Morris to a three-year, $14.8-million contract, breaking the hearts of the fans in Minnesota, where the year before he had led the Twins to the World Series championship.

Here was a pitcher with the most impeccable credentials imaginable as far as intestinal fortitude went,
the kind of guy who all but demanded the ball in a big
game, who battled every inch of the way, who never let
the situation intimidate him, who would only come out
of a game kicking and screaming. Jack Morris wasn't
going to send himself to the showers after five innings
with a lead in the hopes of getting an easy win for his
record. He was going to be there in the tenth inning of
the seventh game of the World Series, pitching with
every bit of strength and every bit of intellect acquired
over fourteen years in the big leagues, just the way he
had done the previous October. With him in a Blue Jay
uniform, the faithful figured a championship was in the
offing.

The next day, they might have felt it was all but in the
bag. Earlier in the fall, Gillick had said that he wasn't
really interested in signing Dave Winfield, who had
become a free agent. After all, Winfield was forty years
old, and even if he had come off a fine offensive season
with the California Angels (28 HRs, 86 RBIs), it was
hard to see him duplicating those numbers at his age.
Plus, Winfield wanted to play in the outfield and the
Jays didn't really think he could play the outfield
anymore, at least on their team, with Carter and White
already in place, and with Maldonado and the hot
young prospect Derek Bell battling for the other spot.

But somewhere along the line, Toronto's thinking
changed. Maybe they realized that what they were
getting in Winfield was not just someone to hit behind
Carter, not just a designated hitter who might play a few
games in the field and drive in eighty runs, but a wealth
of experience and smarts and class, all of which could
only enhance the atmosphere in the clubhouse. And as

for Winfield's motivation, it was clear as day. He had played for eighteen years in the big leagues without playing a day in the minor leagues, and he had never won a World Series. The only time he'd been there, in 1981, he had performed brutally, hitting for an .045 average for the New York Yankees — one hit in twenty-two at-bats. Winfield didn't have much left to prove except that he was capable of leading a team to a championship, and that when the time came he could rise to the occasion. The Jays signed him to a one-year deal.

Roberto knew all too well of Morris's strengths after facing him in the American League Championship Series. Winfield, though, he knew only by reputation, and by the fact that his career overlapped with that of his father. Early on, though, the two developed something of a mutual admiration society — Winfield liked the way Roberto played, and liked his attitude towards the game, and Roberto liked Winfield's breadth of knowledge, his devotion to the craft and his desire to win.

"Winfield is a lot of fun to be with because he knows a lot about the game," Roberto says. "He teaches young kids how to work with baseball. He knows a lot after being in the major leagues for twenty years. He used to play with my Dad, and yet he's still here. He works hard, he's in good shape, he plays like a twenty-nine-year-old guy. Having him on our team was a real plus. He especially meant a lot to me and Joe. This guy is a real leader. Because he was the designated hitter, Winfield was on the bench all the time, so there was always somebody in the dugout yelling for you, not letting the bench get down, keeping people pumped up. And whenever the team went into a slump, we would have a meeting and he would talk and everybody would listen. I know I would listen. There's a guy who has been here for years and years. I talked to him about contracts, about life. He told me to be careful with people, that there are a lot of bad guys out there. He's a real smart person and a great man to talk to.

"The meetings are a family thing. We would talk about everything. Maybe one player has a problem with another player. And there are only players there — no media, no coaches or manager, no anybody. We can talk about it and then let it go. We can resolve the problems. If a guy doesn't run out a ball, it's time to tell him something. You ask guys why they didn't hustle, or why they are pitching that way. There are a lot of things in baseball where you have to give a little push to a player so they can think a little bit more. Winfield was great in those meetings. And he was the one who started the kangaroo court. It's another way of making the players think. For instance, if there's a man on second and nobody out, you have to get the runner over. If you don't, you have to pay a fine. If there's a man on third and less than two out, you have to drive him in. If you don't, you have to pay a fine. Winfield ran it. He was the judge. We had another guy who wrote the notes, the players would tell him what happened, and then it would go to court. You could argue your case. But if the judge said you lose, you had to pay a dollar, or five dollars or ten dollars. We did it as a fun time, and as a way to help the team."

Meanwhile, while the Jays were building towards their strongest run yet at the World Series, back in San Diego, they were still rehashing the trade that a year before had so fundamentally changed the Padres. Fred McGriff had played very, very well indeed in 1991, and given that he was a little younger than Joe Carter, that part of the trade in the long run might well have been in San Diego's favour. But as for the other two parts of the deal — Alomar and Tony Fernandez — it was no contest. Fernandez looked like he might well be on the downside of his career, while Roberto was only getting better. More and more people were beginning to suggest that if he wasn't the best player in the game, he would be soon. Joe McIlvaine had heard all the talk, but he was still standing by his decision.

"Hey, I'm not a dummy," McIlvaine said. "I know how good Alomar is. Robbie was the best player in the trade. There's no question it helped Toronto, but it helped us too. I know what McGriff and Fernandez can do and I also know we didn't see the best of Fernandez either. You'll see a better player this year."

On February 7, Roberto signed a new contract with the Blue Jays: three years for $14 million. Compared to the kind of salaries his father had earned as a ballplayer, it was a staggering sum, but also one that reflected what a great young ballplayer who wasn't yet eligible for free agency could command in 1992. Roberto didn't live an ostentatious life before, and he wasn't likely to begin living one now. He is frugal to a fault, mindful of the financial troubles his father went through after retirement. "I can make a statement now that will still be true twenty years from now," says his endorsement agent, John Boggs. "He will leave the game with some money in the bank. For a guy of his age, he has a terrific amount of smarts about what things he's going to do." What Roberto enjoyed most about the new contract was the feeling that he now had financial security, since even for a talented young ballplayer baseball was an uncertain profession.

"You've got to remember that this could be a one-day

job," Roberto says. "You can get hurt tomorrow and be out of there forever. Suppose you sign a contract for one year and one hundred thousand dollars, you get hurt and that's all you're going to get. If you play ten, maybe fifteen years, you obviously take all the money you can get while you can. People say that we make a lot of money. Well, what about the Michael Jacksons? What about the Rob Lowes? What about the Sylvester Stallones, the Tom Cruises, that little guy that made *Home Alone*? Those guys make millions and millions of dollars. Those are the guys who make a lot of money. We don't make money like that. And Michael Jackson, Madonna, they can be an artist forever. You cannot be a baseball player forever. You have to take advantage of whatever you can now, take as much as you can. That's why I signed the contract, so that I could be secure for life, just in case something happens. I'm still young, but you never know. Look at all of those people who used to play baseball who are suffering now. They didn't save their money right. They made bad investments. Some players declare bankruptcy even after making a million dollars for a few years. That's what people have to realize — it's a tough business."

Heading into spring training in 1992, with Morris and Winfield in the fold, there was a new air of confidence around the proceedings in Dunedin. From day one, the mix in the clubhouse seemed just right. Baseball requires a different emotional tenor than football, where flying sky high once a week will get the job done. Over a 162-game season in a sport that depends far more on fine motor skills than raw aggression, it's important that a team feel comfortable together, that it share common goals. Individuals have to achieve, but they also have to think unselfishly in certain situations.

No part can become greater than the whole. For the Blue Jays in 1992, all of the ambitions, all of the personalities and all of the egos seemed to fit beautifully.

"One bad apple can hurt all the apples," Roberto says. "A manager can put the best nine players out there and if they don't know how to play with each other, they won't win. In football, if you lose on Sunday, you have to wait for seven days to get it out of your system. In this game, you have to be relaxed, you have to have fun. If you don't have fun, you can't do it. You have to accomplish that yourself. Cito can't tell you that you ought to have fun. And I can't go out there and try to do Dave Winfield's job or Joe Carter's job. I have to play for the team. That's what you get paid for. There are people who only think about themselves and their numbers. But they aren't the ones who win."

The Jays opened the season on a glorious, sunny spring afternoon at Tiger Stadium, the fan-friendly old ballpark at the corner of Michigan and Trumbull in Detroit's crumbling core. Morris was on the mound, revisiting the scene of some of his past triumphs while a Tiger, and for the Jays, everything went according to script. Winfield drove in their first run of the season, White played great defence, Olerud hit a home run, as did catcher Pat Borders, Roberto had a hit and scored a run.

Morris, starting on opening day for the thirteenth consecutive season, gave up just three hits over the first eight innings as the Blue Jays built up a 4–0 lead. But in the ninth, Cecil Fielder launched one of his moon shots and it was suddenly 4–1. Cito Gaston walked to the mound, and in most situations with most pitchers, the next move would have been simple: the Blue Jays had the best bullpen one-two in the business with Tom

Henke and Duane Ward; they needed two more outs to seal a victory, with 161 more games to go; Morris had already thrown a pile of pitches; time to hit the showers.

But instead of just handing over the ball and heading for the dugout after a job well done, Morris argued with his manager, pleaded his case. His manager stood, listened, and liked what he heard and left him out there to finish what he'd started.

"If I get to the ninth, then there's only one job to do, and that's finish the ballgame," Morris explained afterwards. "If you're going to bail, bail in the fifth. [Minnesota manager] Tom Kelly understood that, [Detroit manager] Sparky Anderson understood that. When I'm out there, unless there's something wrong with me or I'm dead tired, I'm not going to take myself out."

Morris gave up another home run to Rob Deer, but this time Gaston didn't even bother to visit. He had only his fastball left, and even that was losing its zip, but he hung in, ended up throwing 145 pitches, and completed the game a winner 4–2. His ERA would have been prettier if he'd left when he had the chance, but Jack Morris's brain just doesn't work like that.

Right then and there, the tone was set for a championship season.

10

◇ THE CHAMPIONSHIP SEASON

In the second game of the 1992 season Roberto Alomar served notice of what he had in store. Back at Tiger Stadium after an off-day, the Blue Jays sent Todd Stottlemyre out to face Frank Tanana. With two out and two on in the second inning, Alomar hit his first home run of the year, a shot that put the Jays ahead to stay in what would be a wild 10–9 affair. At the plate and in the field, it would mark the real beginning of his finest season in the big leagues.

Really, there would be no significant dry spells. Unlike 1991, when he started slowly, he was out of the gate fast. In the 20 games remaining in April, Roberto was held without a hit only three times. He finished the month with a .382 average and 19 RBIs, and was named player of the month for both the Blue Jays and the American League.

He was now much more familiar with the pitchers in the league. "Sometimes you're just in the zone," he says. "It's like you're seeing everything right. Every pitch they throw you're going to hit. Anything around the plate you're going to hit hard. Even if they get you out, you're going to hit the ball hard. I just went up there and was seeing the ball well. That was the best month I've ever had in the majors."

May would be almost as good. Roberto hit .314 with 11 RBIs and was again named the Jays player of the month. But he was hardly a one-man show. The Jays were playing very much as a team, and the strong, multi-dimensional batting order helped everyone. The year before, opposing pitchers could relax a bit once they got through the top three or four Toronto hitters. Without a big run producer batting behind him, Joe Carter was pitched around, and even Roberto wasn't seeing a lot of strikes in the number two spot. Adding Dave Winfield to the mix changed that dramatically.

"This year, they had to pitch to Roberto because they didn't want to pitch to me and Winfield," Joe Carter said. "They said we'll let Alomar beat us. And he beat them. I was sitting back watching him and saying, 'I would have rather pitched to me.'"

The Jays were flying early, going 16–7 in April before cooling off to 15–12 in May. On May 24, they fell a half game off the division lead, but that would be the last time all season that they would not have at least a piece of first place. During the first half of the season, the team looked very much like it was ready to live up to its advance billing as the best Toronto side ever. It had great starting pitching and the best bullpen in the majors, it had power, it had speed at the top of the order, it had a nice blend of youth and experience.

It also had great defence, the component most often overlooked by the casual fan, and a happy, cooperative atmosphere in the clubhouse. "I want people to realize from now on that they should be concerned a little more about defence, because it's real important," Roberto says. "When you have good defence behind a pitcher, what's the pitcher going to do? He's going to throw strikes. He says, 'I'm going to throw strikes because I've got guys out there who can catch the ball.' If you've got a good centrefielder, a good rightfielder, a good infield behind you, you can just throw the ball and, wherever they hit it, we have a chance to catch it. We were one of the best defensive teams in baseball, certainly the best one I ever played for.

"I knew from the beginning that we had the team to win it all. We were really looking forward to the season. We made some good moves in the off season and we were looking forward to winning a championship. We had the veterans — Winfield, Morris, Candy. Everyone put in a piece. Day in, day out, it wasn't the same guy who was doing it. Maybe the first month it was Winfield, then it was me, then it was Joe or Candy or Devo. And the pitching was incredible. You need all nine guys to cooperate, and you need the guys on the bench too — Sprague, Derek Bell. The bench, they helped too. Everybody was trying to win. If everybody plays for the team to win, the team will win. If everybody plays for themselves, it won't. The year before, we had a more talented team than Minnesota. But we didn't win because they played better baseball than us. It helps if everyone gets along, because you don't want to play with enemies on the same team. You have to have communication.

"On this team, I didn't see people angry with each other. In San Diego, there was a time when Tony Gwynn and Jack Clark made some comments about each other, and the media made a big deal about it. A little thing became a big thing for the players and the media and the fans. Instead of talking about the game, they were talking about the problem. It didn't hurt me because I was playing my game, but it was hurting some other guys because instead of paying attention to the game they were paying more attention to what was going on in the papers. It was distracting. The Gruber thing wasn't like that. He did some things that people didn't like, but he still went out there and played hard. He hustled and he wanted to win. It was a happy clubhouse. I heard about the way some of the Blue Jay clubhouses were in the past. I wasn't there, so I really don't know what it was like. All I know is that we got along okay."

When adversity did crop up, the team rode it out and adapted. In the second game of the season, rookie Derek Bell, who had won the starting leftfielder job in spring training, broke a bone in his left hand while fouling off a pitch. He would undergo surgery and be lost to the Jays until May 8. For many teams, losing a starter can be disastrous. But for Toronto, Candy Maldonado stepped in and became another important run producer, while playing more than adequately in the field. He was streaky at the plate, but Gaston stuck by him, and in the end he played well enough that when Bell returned, he didn't really have an opportunity to get his job back.

There was also the saga of Dave Stieb, the long-time ace of the Blue Jays starting staff, whose 1991 season was cut in half by a back injury, and who was attempting to come back from off-season surgery. On April 22, he made his first start in a year, and there were high hopes that perhaps he would return to take his place in the rotation: a combination of Morris, Guzman, Key, Stottlemyre and a healthy Stieb would be as powerful as any in baseball. But it wasn't to be. Stieb was ineffective, never returning to his past form, and eventually became a seldom-used member of the bullpen.

"He was working hard," Roberto says. "He really wanted to come back. He was trying his best to go out there and play. You have to respect that. It was good to see him come back, but it wasn't good to see that he didn't have it. But he tried his best."

The fifth starter's spot wasn't really settled until David Cone arrived in August — David Wells, Doug Linton and Pat Hentgen all had starts — but that hardly slowed the team's momentum. By the time the All Star break arrived, Toronto's record was 53–34, and they led the division by four games. Kelly Gruber's brash pre-season prediction that the Jays would be fifteen or sixteen games up in the AL East by the time the season was done didn't seem that far-fetched. The Boston Red Sox were in decline and the Baltimore Orioles were playing over their heads, and could expected to fall back. The Jays might not hit real competition until the playoffs.

Roberto's first-half numbers were sensational. He was hitting .323 to lead the team, and was batting well from both sides of the plate — .363 righthanded, .306 lefthanded. He had stolen eighteen bases, trailing team leader Devon White by one, and in the field he had made just four errors. He was voted to the American League All Star team for the second year in a row, he was playing in the game for the third year in a row, and this time it would be special for several reasons. His friend Joe Carter was selected to the team (in fact all four of the players in the Big Trade — Alomar, Carter, Fred McGriff and Tony Fernandez — played in the game), as was Guzman, who finished the first half 11–2 with a 2.11 ERA, and the player the Jays had traded for him, Los Angeles second baseman Mike Sharperson. The game would be played at Jack Murphy Stadium in San Diego, where Roberto had begun his major league career, and where he still had many friends and fans, and maybe a point to make with the Padres' management.

"That was the first time I'd played there since I was traded. It was great to go out there and see the fans. We just went there to have some fun."

Sandy Jr. was also there, voted in by the fans despite an injury-marred first half of the season. "I knew I didn't deserve to be in the All Star Game," he says. "I hadn't played enough. But you have to take it when you can because there are some years where you're having a great year and they're going to vote for somebody else. I wasn't the first player in that situation. It's all a popularity contest. If you have a first great year and you get all this publicity, that helps. Plus if you're nice to the fans and you sign autographs, that's going to help you too. The All Star Game is for the people and the people voted me in."

"I felt good about that," Maria says. "Sandy did not play, but the fans voted for him anyway. They like my kids. I tell my kids, you have to spend time with the fans. Then they'll stay with you. I see many players who don't like the people around them. I don't like that."

And Nestor Pabon would be there as well, along with his sister-in-law Carmen. The trip was Roberto's gift to the man who was like his second father, and to the neighbour who was like his second mother. Nestor was terminally ill, and so it was an especially emotional time for all.

"Nestor treated me real good when I was a young kid," Roberto says. "He used to take me to his house, take care of me, he used to give me some money whenever we were going through hard times. He helped a lot. I knew he was going to die of liver cancer. He told my Mom one time that he wanted to see me in the World Series. I knew he wasn't going to make it that long. So I took him to the All Star Game. Carmen, my neighbour, came with him. She's like my mom. I told her I was going to give her a present. Sometimes you want to pay someone back for what they've done for you. Nestor wasn't talking that much. He laughed a lot but he talked real soft. I found out that he died just before the playoffs started. They didn't want to tell me but I heard from somebody else. I felt sad, but I felt happy too because he had suffered so much. It's not good to have that happen to a person that you love. It's not good to stay here suffering."

In the All Star Game, Roberto put on a show for his guests. He singled in the second inning, his first hit in an All Star Game, and then proceeded to steal second and third. The pitcher was Tom Glavine of the Atlanta Braves and the catcher was Benito Santiago of the Padres, who grew up down the road from Roberto in Puerto Rico. "I didn't steal the bases off Benito," Roberto said. "I stole them off the pitcher. He had a slow motion." He didn't realize that he had tied a record by stealing two bases in the All Star Game — never mind in a single inning. "If I'd known that," he said, "I would have stolen home."

The Blue Jays reassembled at the Seattle Kingdome after the break, ready to resume their triumphal march to the division title, and for a while they did just that, winning three of four from the Mariners to keep their lead at four games. Juan Guzman won one of those games, throwing seven shutout innings for the win. But he left his next start after three innings with a sore shoulder, and on August 5 was placed on the fifteen-day disabled list. "When Guzman went out of the rotation, we weren't the same," Roberto says. "We felt like we were missing something. It's like when you have twenty dollars and you lose five and you're left with fifteen, it doesn't feel the same as twenty. The way he was going in the beginning, we were missing something important when he was hurt."

Toronto didn't only lose its best starting pitcher, it also watched the rest of its rotation — with the exception of Jack Morris — go south for much of August. Jimmy Key was 1–4 with a 6.25 ERA. David Wells was 1–4 with a 13.14 ERA. And the Orioles, riding their hot young pitching staff, refused to give any ground. The Team of Destiny was suddenly fighting tooth and nail for first place, and all of the demons of the past resurfaced. How could this club, with this much talent, possibly blow the division? On August 12, the Orioles came into the SkyDome, beat the Blue Jays 3–0, and the division lead was down to two games. The next night, Baltimore won 11–4, and the lead was down to one.

"You're going to go through a struggle," Roberto says. "A few pitchers were hurt, and the other pitchers were struggling a bit. They knew we needed another starting pitcher, and they went out and found one."

The Jays had actually pushed their lead up to four games, and then watched it shrink back to two and a half, by the time Pat Gillick made his move. David Cone, the National League strike out leader and a consensus choice as one of the best two or three pitchers in baseball, would be a free agent in the off-season. His team, the New York Mets, were going nowhere, and figuring that they were going to lose Cone anyway, were looking to strike a deal. The price wasn't that steep — infielder Jeff Kent, who had played well subbing for the injured Kelly Gruber, and fine minor league prospect Ryan Thompson — but considering the Jays were really just renting Cone for the final two months of the season, it wasn't exactly a bargain, either. The deal would prove to be a classic stretch drive addition, the kind of trade that has historically propelled teams to championships.

"That was a great move," Roberto says. "I couldn't believe it when I heard about it. When I was in San Diego, I knew that he was one of the best pitchers in baseball. He was great for us. When we got him, I felt like that was the point where I knew we would win.

"It was still a good race. Baltimore had a good pitching staff and Milwaukee was playing great. We didn't put pressure on ourselves. We had a meeting at the beginning of September and said we have the ability to play the game. We have a lot of ability here. We have a good team. Let's go out there and play. That's what we did. We beat Baltimore in Toronto, and that was a big plus for us. We got two games out of them. And after that we split with Milwaukee. That was good too."

Toronto's lead would shrink to a half game in the first week of September. But after that, Baltimore would finally end its charge, and Milwaukee's late drive would fall just short.

Along the way, Jack Morris would become the first Blue Jay pitcher to win twenty games. Dave Winfield would change forever the sound of baseball in the SkyDome, when he implored the fans to make more noise and they responded as they never had before.

There was also the matter of The Stare. During a game in early September, Roberto uncharacteristically complained to reporters that someone on the Blue Jay bench, someone on his own team, had been giving him the evil eye as he walked to the dugout after an at-bat, and he didn't much like it. It would later be revealed that the starer was none other than Toronto bench coach Gene Tenace, who had managed the team when Gaston's back flared up in 1991.

"It wasn't a big deal," Roberto says. "I thought I was doing my job, but he liked me to play the game a little differently. I just let him know that I would not play the game differently. They know I have power, they know I can pull the ball, and they want me to hit away with a man on second because I was one of the best hitters on the team. They wanted me to swing the bat and not give up the out. But for me, if I've got a man on second base with nobody out, I'm going to move him up because my job is to put that guy to third base. I just want to do my job. If I'm hitting second, that's why I was thinking like that. If I was hitting third or I was hitting fifth, it would be different. Maybe I'd swing the bat a little bit more. Tenace was trying to get me to play the game differently. It was just something that I wanted to say and get out of my system. It felt good to do that. We talked about it a little bit afterwards. Gene is really a great guy."

The Jays clinched the division title on the second to last day of the season. Juan Guzman threw eight shutout innings against Detroit, gave up just one hit and struck out nine. The celebration afterwards was slightly muted compared to the party following past Toronto triumphs. This time, no one would be satisfied just to be in the playoffs — not the players, not the front office and especially not the fans.

Roberto's end-of-the-season statistics provided plenty of evidence for those who argued that he might now be the best player in all of baseball. He hit for a career high .310 average, with a career best 76 runs batted in. He hit .354 with runners in scoring position, .444 with the bases loaded. He reached base in 128 of the 152 games he played and scored 105 runs. He walked 87 times, the most in his career and the third highest total ever for a Blue Jay. He stole 49 bases, including 13 steals of third. His fielding percentage was a career best .993, second highest in the American League. He made just five errors, and his range at second base was unmatched by anyone.

Putting those numbers together with Alomar's nearly flawless baseball instincts, it was hard to imagine a more complete player — a fact made all the more remarkable because he was only twenty-four years old. By the end of the 1992 season, the baseball world knew that this was a very special athlete.

"This kid has a chance to be a Hall-of-Famer," says Cito Gaston. "I think Roberto's getting better every year."

"It's been an honour playing with a talent like Robbie," says Candy Maldonado. "His God-given ability, the way he conducts himself, I think it shows a lot about his character. It was unique to be right beside him and see a player who, to me, compares to a Michael Jordan in basketball, a guy who creates so many things on the field. It's scary that at age twenty-four, everything has fallen into place, and yet you know that he still has a long way to go."

"For me," says Carlos Baerga, "Robbie right now is one of the most complete players in the big leagues. I can compare him with Barry Bonds and Kirby Puckett and Ken Griffey Jr. Those three players can do everything — they can field, they can throw, they are intelligent in what they do and they can hit for power and RBIs."

"The scary thing is that he's going to get better," says Tony Gwynn. "He's just starting to get in that groove. Before it's all over he's going to win a batting title and he's going to lead the league in stolen bases some year. That's just my opinion."

"I think he can be a guy who can go down in the record books," Deacon Jones says. "I think he can be consistent stealing a lot of bases, maybe fifty a year. He's going to hit for average. I don't see him going into any prolonged slumps, because if he does struggle, he'll get out of it because he can lay down a bunt or take a walk."

"I think you're looking at one of the greatest who has ever played his position," says Luis Rosa. "In the annals of Puerto Rican history, they will always say that he was born for the game and that he lives for the game."

"You see Tony Gwynn, you see Roberto Alomar, you see Barry Bonds, Ryne Sandberg," says Jack McKeon. "You go through the major leagues and you can pick out seven or eight guys who have it. Early on you could see that Roberto had the tools to win a Gold Glove, and he's done that. I think he's going to win a batting title or two before he's done. I think he's the best player, the most talented player, in the American League."

"You just take Robbie Alomar's name, and then put three dots after it," Joe Carter says. "He just has unlimited potential. Right now, he's the best all-around player in baseball."

"When Robbie puts his best effort into the game," says his father, "you very seldom will see a better player."

Game one of the American League Championship Series would be played in Toronto, and the anticipation there was sky high. The Oakland Athletics, champions of the American League West, were a formidable team, led by the power hitting of Mark McGwire and the non-pareil reliever Dennis Eckersley. But they weren't the As of 1989 who had humiliated Toronto in the playoffs — Jose Canseco was gone, and Rickey Henderson appeared to have lost a step and lost some of his fire. Toronto, with its deep pitching staff and its potent offence would enter the series a clear favourite.

"Maybe it was a little bit different this year, because we had to win this time," Roberto says. "We couldn't lose like last year. I felt like we were going to beat Minnesota — everybody felt that way — but we learned that you can't take anything for granted. This year we had more power. We had Winfield, Joe, Candy and Olerud. We had more of everything. It was a good team in all ways. And we had more confidence. We thought we were the best team in baseball."

Unlike the ill-fated 1991 ALCS, there would be no controversy about which pitcher would start the series for the Jays. The Blue Jays would of course send Jack Morris out to pitch the first game. He had won twenty-one times during the regular season, and though his ERA was on the high side, his competitive nature had always served him well in the post-season. A lack of tenacity had been regarded as one of the Jays' problems in the past. With Morris on the mound, the desire to win would never be an issue. After that would come Cone and Guzman, while Jimmy Key and Todd Stottlemyre would await the call in the bullpen. No team in baseball — with the possible exception of the National League West champion Atlanta Braves — could match that kind of starting talent.

Oakland countered with Dave Stewart, who was coming off a year that, statistically, had not been one of his better ones. But, like Morris, he was known for his big-game performances — Stewart had never lost in the post-season. After that they would send up Mike Moore, Ron Darling and Bob Welch, all of them talented but none of them a sure thing, especially in the playoffs.

"Morris is the kind of guy who tries to win every game he is pitching," Roberto says. "And Dave Stewart is the one who tries to intimidate you with his look, his stare. When he does that I don't look at him. I just look at his arm so he doesn't intimidate me. He's a competitor too. They're really similar pitchers. They both throw split finger fastballs. They like to move their fastballs. They both throw sliders. They go right after hitters — they don't care who it is. When they're ahead, they'll go after you, and when they're behind they still want to throw their game. With Morris, you have to be aggressive at the plate. You can't get behind in the count. And Morris is the kind of guy, who, if you make a good play behind him, he gets excited on the mound. That gets you excited too. It's good to have him on the mound cheering for you. Stewart's just a bit different. Sometimes he starts with a split finger, sometimes he starts with a fastball or a slider. It depends on what the score is. If they're up 5–0 or 6–0 he'll go right after you. If the score's 1–1 with a runner like me, he won't want to walk me.

"We knew it was going to be a pitcher's battle. We just didn't score any runs for Morris. Morris pitched a great game but he made one mistake. He made the right decision on the pitch, but if you don't throw that pitch where you want it, you're going to get hurt. He wasn't getting the location. He was leaving the ball up. You very rarely see Morris walking a guy, and he was walking guys. He made one big mistake. He threw a hanging slider on top of the plate and Harold Baines hit it pretty good over the fence."

That home run, with the score tied 3–3 heading into the ninth inning, sent the entire city of Toronto into shock. Those who weren't criticizing Gaston for leaving Morris in too long were criticizing Morris for earning a big salary and then not being perfect when it mattered most.

In fact, the only place in town where there was no hint of panic was in the Blue Jays locker room. "It was only one game," Roberto says. "We went inside and said, 'we'll get them tomorrow.'"

Game two would match Cone against Oakland's Moore. "Mike Moore throws the same pitches that Dave Stewart throws. He moves the ball around real good. And David Cone's got a great slider. I don't think the American League guys knew Cone very well. He was getting good location, and if David Cone gets good location he will be tough to hit. He threw great in that game and we scored a few runs for him."

The key play actually turned out to be one that wasn't made at all. In the top of the fifth with no score, and both pitchers in control, the Athletics had Willie Wilson on second and Mike Bordick on first with one out with Walt Weiss at bat. Cone's problems holding runners were well known to the As. On the night they would wind up with six stolen bases — two of them on what would be Wilson and Bordick's double steal. To compound the Jays' problems, Cone's pitch was wild, glancing off Pat Borders' shin pad and rolling towards the Toronto dugout. Borders ran after the ball, and had a chance to grab it before it fell into the dugout. Instead he hesitated, and let it fall as Wilson was about to cross the plate, and for a moment just about everyone in the stadium was confused as to what was going on.

"Alfredo Griffin was the one who was yelling in the

dugout," Roberto says. "If you let it go, it's a dead ball and the runner has to go back to third base." And that's exactly what happened. Even though he would have scored easily, Wilson was sent back to third and Bordick back to second. Cone then struck out Weiss and Rickey Henderson to end the inning without giving up a run.

The Jays scored two in the bottom of the fifth on a home run by Kelly Gruber, who at least temporarily got the fans off his back and on side with his first hit of the series. They never trailed after that. In the ninth, with Toronto up 3–0 on another run driven in by Gruber, Ruben Sierra tripled off Cone, and then Baines singled off Tom Henke to drive him in. But then Henke retired the next three batters for his first save of the post season. The game was over, the series was tied, and Torontonians were breathing a little easier.

The series moved to Oakland for game three, with Ron Darling starting for the As against Toronto's Juan Guzman. Twice during the regular season, Darling had pitched brilliantly against Toronto. "Darling pitched great games against us — almost two no hitters. He had good control in those games. But this time, he didn't have control like he did before. Sometimes you put a little bit of pressure on yourself. He left the ball up and we hit it pretty good."

Guzman wasn't at his best either, pitching in and out of trouble during his six innings. The Toronto bullpen was also uncharacteristically erratic. Duane Ward in particular had an awful inning of work, giving up two runs on three hits and a walk.

But this time, Toronto's bats — and Oakland's three errors — were the difference. In the second inning, Winfield reached base on an error, took third on a wild pitch, and then scored on Candy Maldonado's single to make it 1–0. Then in the fourth, Roberto went deep off Darling.

"It was 3–1, so I wanted to try and hit the ball hard. I knew he was going to come with a fastball and I knew he was going to come outside. So I was trying to hit the ball the other way hard and I did.

"Candy had a home run in the fifth and Manuel Lee hit a triple and we scored two runs in the seventh. Everyone was doing something. That triple was a key hit for us. When you've got a guy like Darling over there, and the way he pitched against us during the year, you have to score some runs. We knew that we had one of our best pitchers on the mound. So if we score some runs for Juan, we know he's going to be a little bit more comfortable on the mound."

The final score was 7–5 Toronto, a messy win, a win with lots of nervous moments, but a win nonetheless. The Blue Jays had recaptured the home field advantage, and were just two victories away from the World Series.

Then came the dramatics of game four. "That was the turning point in the playoff," Joe Carter says. After the stunning comeback victory, Toronto had the series very much in control, just as they had in 1985 against Kansas City before the great collapse. Still, this was a different kind of team, and most expected them to go in for the kill in game five, with Cone up to face a band of dispirited As on the verge of elimination.

Instead, it was Toronto that seemed to have mentally let down, and it was Oakland starter Dave Stewart who rose to the occasion, along with Toronto's old nemesis, Rickey Henderson, whose running gave the Jays fits all afternoon. The As scored early, on Ruben Sierra's two-run first inning homer, and in the fifth inning they all but put it away, pulling ahead 6–1. The final score was 6–2, and the series was heading back to Toronto.

"We knew that even if we lost that game, we would still be back in Toronto up 3–2," Roberto says. "I thought we were going to win that game, though, but Stewart pitched a great game and they played great baseball. Maybe that was just their game to win. I hit the ball hard twice with men on base. If those balls had gone through, we might have tied the game. Maybe we were meant to win it in Toronto. At least we knew that we were going home, we were going back to Canada."

That day, after the game, Roberto summed up the way his team was feeling. "I wasn't here when they didn't win in the past," he said. "I just want to be here in the present when we win the big one so we won't have to hear anymore about the past."

The SkyDome was a madhouse for game six, charged by a wild mix of emotions including excitement and anticipation and an underlying sense of dread. A year before, the Blue Jays had come home in position to knock off the Twins and advance to the World Series, and those with longer memories could conjure up images of Jim Sundberg's windblown triple in 1985, and the letdown that ensued. Toronto had to win just one of two at home, and with Juan Guzman and Jack Morris the scheduled starters, it was hard not to like their chances. But Toronto Blue Jay fans had come to know better than just about anyone that it was best not to count your chickens.

The team, though, wasn't suffering from the tight collar syndrome that may have preyed on Blue Jays past. "They had the pressure, not us," Roberto say. "We were at home and we were up 3–2. And they had the pressure of the fans. The fans were great to us. They made a lot of noise, and that put a lot of pressure on the Oakland As. That can make a difference. The visitors feel like they're playing against the crowd and the home team has a little bit more enthusiasm for the game."

Game six would turn out to be all ecstasy and very little agony for the Blue Jay partisans. Guzman mowed down the As in order in the top of the first. Then Devon White, leading off the game for Toronto, lofted a flyball to left that Rickey Henderson saw, got under, and dropped. Roberto struck out, but Joe Carter followed with a home run to straightaway centre. "Joe hit a home run in the first inning, and from that point on everybody woke up and played a great game." In the third, the Jays finished the job: Roberto singled and stole second, and after Carter struck out and Winfield walked, John Olerud hit a ground rule double. Candy Maldonado followed with a home run to make it 6–0, and the celebration began. The game ended 9–2, and the Blue Jays and their fans knew it was official: Toronto had won the pennant. Roberto was named the most valuable player in the ALCS, after hitting .423 for the series.

That night, the Atlanta Braves beat the Pittsburgh Pirates with two out, ninth inning heroics in the seventh game of the National League Championship Series. It would be Toronto and Atlanta — one franchise that has never won the championship, the other that has never won it since moving to its home in Georgia — vying for the 1992 World Series.

"We felt real happy, because it was the first time a Canadian team was going to the World Series," Roberto says. "But we knew we had one more step to go."

11

 THE FALL CLASSIC

The souvenir sellers circled Fulton County Stadium in the morning, staking out their places. By early afternoon, a few fans were starting to mill about, many of them in some kind of mock-Indian wear or another, almost all of them carrying the ubiquitous foam rubber tomahawk. An hour before game time, the crowds outside had swelled, the anticipation level was high, the chanting had begun. *Oooh . . . Oooh . . . Oh Oh Oh Oooooh.* All great sporting events have a certain atmosphere that precedes them: the Super Bowl, the Olympic Games, a big fight in Las Vegas. The World Series has its own air, charged for sure, but relaxed in the same way the game itself is relaxed. Nothing is going to happen in an instant, nothing is going to be won or lost for a few days yet. This is but a beginning following other baseball beginnings: the first day of spring training, the first day of the season, the first game after the All Star break, the first game of the September pennant race, the first game of the League Championships. There is still time to stretch and eat a hot dog and look around and enjoy what's happening.

But of course this is also The Show, and for Atlanta and their owner, the cable television mogul Ted Turner, there is the added sense of having been here once, of having lost in heartbreaking circumstances, and of hoping against hope that it won't happen again. The Braves had gone back to Minnesota in 1991 needing one win in two games to clinch the title. Two extra-inning games and two guys named Kirby Puckett and Jack Morris made sure that didn't happen. The Twins couldn't make it back this year, though. The Braves, the best team in the National League all season, did return by winning their division and beating Pittsburgh in the NLCS. That last win came in such a fashion — a two-out, two-run, bottom of the ninth, seventh-game single that turned defeat into victory — that those who saw signs in the random workings of the universe could have believed the Braves were destined to triumph.

By contrast, for the Blue Jays and for Toronto's fans, the World Series was still a novel experience. Morris had been there of course, as had Winfield — though he'd probably rather forget his performance for the Yankees in 1981. And Candy Maldonado had been on the losing end with the San Francisco Giants in 1989. But for the rest of the team and for the faithful, it was a time for soaking up the sights and sounds and marvelling at what it was like to still be playing ball when most of the baseball world was already working on its golf game.

The Blue Jays lineup, as engraved in stone as the Ten Commandments for most of the season, would have to be altered slightly, at least for the games played in

Atlanta. In the National League park, National League rules would apply, and so pitchers would have to hit for themselves. Designated hitter Dave Winfield's bat, though, was too valuable to leave on the bench, and so Cito Gaston came up with an NL shuffle: Winfield would play rightfield. Against lefthanders, Joe Carter would move to first base and John Olerud would sit. Against righthanders, Carter would move to leftfield, and Candy Maldonado would sit.

The Jays' braintrust, after assessing the performances during the ALCS, also shuffled their starting pitchers. The three-man rotation would become a four-man rotation, with lefthander Jimmy Key in the extra spot to neutralize some of Atlanta's lefthanded power. The first three pitchers would stay the same — Morris, Cone, Guzman — but if there were to be a game seven, Guzman would now do the honours for Toronto.

Atlanta manager Bobby Cox, still beloved in Hogtown for his years as the Jays field boss, countered with his big three: Tom Glavine, John Smoltz and Steve Avery. Glavine, Morris's opposite number in game one, was the 1991 Cy Young Award winner who was coming off a second consecutive twenty-win season, with a stellar 2.76 ERA. But he was also pitching on the heels of a none-too-successful NLCS, and was hearing whispers that he might be incapable of winning the big one.

By the time game one was finished, there wasn't much whispering to be heard. Glavine's performance was the story of the game: he gave up just four hits, faced only thirty Toronto batters, and allowed one run, on Joe Carter's fourth inning homer.

"I faced Glavine before when I was in San Diego," Roberto says. "He throws a lot of change-ups, he keeps the ball outside. He throws good in and out. He was throwing the ball outside in that game and the umpires were giving him a little more than we thought they would. He was keeping the ball on the outside corner. It was a problem that most of the guys hadn't seen him before. But he had changed since the first time I saw him, too. He was a lot better.

"The other thing was that the strike zone was funny for the whole series except for the last game. It was a big zone. The last game was a good zone because John Shulock did a great job. But the other guys didn't call good games and they missed a few plays in the series that could have cost games."

For Morris, the story was the same as it had been in the American League Championship Series. He pitched pretty much as he had pitched during the regular season, when his ERA was over four, and where he also received great run support. But in the playoffs, the runs didn't materialize for him, and he seemed prone to making the wrong pitch at the wrong time. "He pitched great but we just didn't hit for him," Roberto says. "Morris just made one mistake and that was the game." The mistake, a fastball higher than Morris had wanted it and right down the middle, was hit out of the park by Atlanta catcher Damon Berryhill with two men on in the sixth inning. That broke a string of eighteen consecutive scoreless World Series innings for Morris, and it made Berryhill — who was the regular catcher only by virtue of the fact that the Braves starter Greg Olson had broken his ankle earlier in the season — the first of the Series' unlikely heroes.

And so the Jays found themselves in a familiar position — down one game to none with Morris under fire, since he still had yet to win in the post-season for Toronto.

Game two began with the inverted flag incident, when a U.S. Marine colour guard marched on the field, stood through the anthems, and then marched off, all the while holding the Canadian flag upside down. "We didn't notice it," Roberto says. "I heard about it after the game." The real bad news for Canada, though, was that John Smoltz looked unhittable. He struck out five of the first Blue Jays he faced, and when Atlanta scored a run on a David Cone wild pitch in the second inning, it was easy to believe they wouldn't need anything more.

"Smoltz is a different pitcher," Roberto says. "He throws harder than Glavine. He has a good curveball and good control. He throws strikes. He pitched a great game and Cone pitched a great game and we made some good plays in the field."

In the fourth inning, it looked like the Jays might be about to even the score. Roberto walked to lead off the inning, advanced to second on a wild pitch, and then moved to third when Dave Winfield grounded out. The first pitch to the next batter, John Olerud, squirted past Berryhill, and bounced off to his right. Roberto immediately charged towards the plate, sliding head first, with his hands extended towards home. Meanwhile Berryhill retrieved the ball and flipped it underhand to Smoltz, who was covering. It was a close play, but the television replays showed clearly that Roberto's hand was on the plate before Smoltz applied the tag.

Unfortunately, home plate umpire Mike Reilly didn't see it that way. He called Roberto out.

"That was a terrible call at home plate," Roberto says. "I just don't know how he could have called me out. I was upset because the play was in front of him. Right in front of his face. And he missed the call. That call could have cost us the game. I just said to him, 'you missed the call.' That's all I said. Really."

He didn't say it, really. He screamed it. But not loud enough or long enough to risk ejection.

The Braves went up 2–0 in their half of the fourth, before Toronto rallied back to tie the game in the top of the fifth, with Cone and Devon White driving in the runs with singles. Neon Deion Sanders put the Braves back in the lead in their half of the inning. He singled, stole second off Cone (who would give up five steals on the night), went to third when Pat Borders' throw skipped into centrefield, and then scored on a Dave Justice single. "Sanders showed me a lot in that series," Roberto says. "He can play the game. He has a lot of talent for the game. He's a great player.

"Atlanta were going to run all night because the motions of the pitchers were slow, and they're going to take advantage of that. They have some good runners on that team.There's nothing much you can do. If the catcher makes a perfect throw to second base, maybe we can get him. But you steal the base on the pitcher."

By the end of the inning, the Braves were up 4–2, and Smoltz still looked strong.

Toronto didn't get to him until the eighth. With one out, Roberto doubled — his first hit of the World Series. Carter and Winfield singled, and it was 4–3. But then Cox called for Jeff Reardon, one of the greatest relievers in baseball history with 357 career saves recorded in New York, Montreal, Minnesota, Boston and — since August 1991 — Atlanta. "He doesn't have the same velocity that he used to have," Roberto says, "and that night he was hanging pitches. If he'd thrown the pitch where he wanted to, nobody would have hit it out. But he threw it in the wrong spot."

In fact, first he threw his pitches in the right spot, popping up Olerud and then striking out Kelly Gruber, looking, to end the Blue Jays threat in the eighth. But in the top of the ninth, in position to close out the game and put the Braves up 2–0 in the Series, Reardon faltered. With one out, Derek Bell was sent in to hit for the shortstop, Manuel Lee. "Derek had a great at-bat when he walked. You see all the guys were doing everything together to win. Derek's still a young guy. He's going to learn about this game, and he's going to be a better player as he gets older. He has great abilities. He could be one of the best outfielders in the game. He's got the tools." The pitch Bell took for ball four could well have been strike three, but for a change the erratic umpiring worked in favour of the Blue Jays.

The next hitter was Ed Sprague, a back-up catcher and third baseman, hitting in the pitcher's spot. Reardon threw him a big, fat, not particularly swift fastball right down the middle of the plate with his first pitch and Sprague got all of it, hitting it over the fence in left and putting the Jays up 5–4.

That meant it was Tom Henke time, and as usual he came through, though it was hardly automatic. With Jane Fonda praying in the stands next to her hubby, Ted Turner, Henke hit Ron Gant, gave up a walk to Sanders, and then faced Terry Pendleton, the possessor of a .387 average with runners in scoring position. But Pendleton wasn't patient, going after the first pitch and popping it up in foul territory, where Gruber caught it for the third out.

Just to punctuate the victory, Gruber did a little tomahawk chop of his own, a message to the Braves and the Atlanta fans that the Blue Jays would not be intimidated.

The Series came to Toronto for game three, and inside the SkyDome Canadians and Americans made peace over the great flag incident before the first pitch was thrown. The noise was overwhelming, the loudest Toronto crowd for anything, anytime, and sitting in the stands, Maria and Sandy Sr. couldn't believe it.

"I was in Toronto for three games and it was fantastic," Maria says. "I never imagined such a crowd. There were so many people. People outside, people inside the hotel. And the enthusiasm . . . I enjoyed it over there, but I was nervous all the time."

Once again, the pitching match-up was intriguing. Steve Avery, the Braves' lefthander, had been a sensation in 1991, but had seen his record fall from 18–8 to 11–11 in 1992 — though his ERA actually dropped from 3.38 to 3.20. He was a hard thrower who, despite the advantage of being lefthanded, had trouble holding runners on. He would face Guzman, who through his playoff performances had convinced anyone who needed convincing that he was now the ace of the Toronto staff.

The first three innings were scoreless. In the fourth, the Braves seemed on the verge of a breakthrough. Deion Sanders singled, Terry Pendleton singled, and there were men on first and second with none out and David Justice at the plate. Justice saw a pitch he liked and got just about all of it. It rocketed on a line towards straightaway centrefield, and if it wasn't a triple, it had to be a home run. The baserunners were playing halfway on this one. So sure were they that the ball wasn't going to be caught that they began their sprint for home.

They had underestimated the athletic abilities of Devon White. Looking over his shoulder at the ball, he ran full out towards the wall. At the warning track he lept, snared it, and smashed hard into the fence just to the left of the 400-foot sign. He didn't drop it on impact, and instead spun and fired the ball back to the infield.

"It was a great catch. Devo makes great catches all the time," Roberto says. "I always say that Devo's the best I've ever seen in the game. Watching him every day, I think that there are only three guys who can play like that: Ken Griffey Jr. and Devo and Kirby Puckett. But Devo's number one for me. He's made so many great catches that it's hard to say which one is the best. I remember one he made in Cleveland last year, when he jumped over the fence, and he made one in Milwaukee that was great, too. Devo runs good and he makes all the plays all the time. I knew he was going to catch it. I've got confidence in him. I didn't know it was going to be that tough, but I knew he was going to catch it.

"That play shows you the value of defence. If we didn't play good defence, we wouldn't have won the World Series. The press doesn't think about that, but it's true. They write about how Devon White was hitting one-something in the Series, Roberto Alomar was hitting one-something, Joe Carter was hitting two-fifty-something. But if you play good defence and you get good pitching, you're going to win a lot of games. Who cares about hits? This is only four, six, seven games we're talking about. What he did that day was like an RBI for us. They would have scored at least one run. I got a hit in the ninth inning, I stole second and went to third. I only got one hit but I got the game-winning run."

As the ball was coming in, Roberto stood in front of home plate in cut-off position. "When he hit the ball I was looking back and forth between Devo and the infield. I saw Pendleton running, and he was already past second base and Deion was around third base. When he threw me the ball, I just automatically threw to first base, because I knew how far off the runner was. Then the other runner, Sanders, got caught in the rundown and Kelly tagged him. He tagged Deion Sanders on the foot. I saw it because I was in front of the plate. It was a triple play. I saw it. He tagged him. It was a triple play. There was another mistake by an umpire in the Series."

Again, replays seemed to show that the umpire had blown the call, that Gruber had made the tag for the triple play. But in the confusion on the basepaths, unbeknownst to Roberto, Pendleton had actually passed Sanders, making him automatically out, and making the throw to first meaningless. The Jays seemed to get the triple play the hard way, even though they didn't get credit for it. They could have had it simply by flipping the ball to second and touching the bag.

In the bottom of the fourth inning, Roberto grounded out, leaving him just 1–11 at the plate for the Series. But Joe Carter followed with his second World Series home run, into the auxiliary press box set up in the leftfield bleachers, and it was 1–0 Toronto.

The Braves couldn't solve Guzman until the sixth. With one out, Deion Sanders doubled to right. Terry Pendleton followed with an infield single to shortstop — a ball that Manuel Lee fielded and threw to third, trying unsuccessfully to nail the lead runner. Justice then singled to right to make it 1–1. In the top of the eighth, the Braves went up 2–1 when Otis Nixon hit a line drive through Kelly Gruber's glove that should have been caught, stole a base, and eventually scored on Lonnie Smith's single.

The error did nothing to endear Gruber to the

Toronto fans, who had long been on his back because of stories that he had been malingering during the regular season, claiming an injury and then going water-skiing while on the disabled list. His production had tailed off dramatically since his breakthrough season in 1990, and aside from his ALCS home run, he had been having a dismal playoff at the plate and was 0–23 in the World Series to that point — the longest hitless streak in a single post-season in baseball history.

He responded by stepping up in the bottom of the eighth, working Avery to a full count, and then hitting the ball over the leftfield fence to tie the game.

"People always ask me what kind of a guy Gruber is," Roberto says. "I say he is a nice guy. Maybe he can be something else to the media, but he is nice to me. I'm not in the media. I was his teammate. I respect all my teammates. My teammates are my family. All they have to do is go out there and do their job.

"Sometimes, other players got on him because he didn't know how to play with injuries. But Kelly's the only one who knows whether he's injured or not. In this game you have to worry about yourself. You can't worry about the other guy.

"I don't believe the story about him water skiing because I didn't see him. You're in the public eye when you're a baseball player. There are a lot of things that are said that aren't true and a lot of things that are said that are true. How can you prove to me that he was doing that? I didn't believe that, but I think some of the other guys believed it."

The game went to the bottom of the ninth still tied at two. The SkyDome crowd was primed for victory in the Jays' final at-bat, and when Roberto singled off Avery to lead off, they knew the chances of that happening had just gone from slim to very good. "He threw me a fastball and I hit it up the middle," Roberto says. "Then they knew it would be easy for me to steal the base off Avery because he has a real slow delivery." Jimy Williams, acting for Cox, who had been ejected in the top of the ninth for throwing a helmet on the field (a tantrum prompted by a questionable strike call), lifted Avery and brought in fireballer Mark Wohlers. The change in pitchers didn't change Roberto's running game: he immediately stole second.

Carter walked and then Winfield, the clean-up hitter, did what clean-up hitters aren't asked to do very often: he put down a perfect sacrifice bunt, advancing the runners. With Alomar at third and Carter at second, the first real managerial chess game of the Series began. John Olerud, a lefthander, was scheduled up next, and first base was empty. Williams/Cox opted to bring in a lefthander, Mike Stanton. Cito Gaston countered with pinch hitter Ed Sprague, the hero of game two, a righthander. The Braves had Stanton walk Sprague intentionally to load the bases. Then, with Candy Maldonado due up, they brought in Jeff Reardon, victimized once already in the Series. Reardon had retired Maldonado eleven of the thirteen times he'd faced him in his career.

"It had been an up and down year for Candy," Roberto says. "After Derek Bell got hurt, they gave him the position and he started playing good baseball. He won the job. He's got a lot of power. He's a strong guy and he's a good situation hitter."

In this situation, with the outfield drawn in, where a long flyball or perhaps even a groundball would win the game, Maldonado looked sick on the first two pitches, both of them curveballs that he swung right through.

If it worked twice, Reardon figured, it would probably work again. He threw a third curve that hung out over the plate like a ball on a tee. Maldonado launched it to centrefield — a harmless flyball out in other circumstances, the killing blow in these.

Roberto loped home from third with the winning run, to the roar of the SkyDome crowd. Along the way, he performed a little tomahawk chop, just as Gruber had at the end of game two. "When we played against them, they always gave us the chop," Roberto says. "So why not do the same? They did it before to us. Everywhere we go in their city we get the chop. All through the game we get the chop. I guess we just learned from them."

As was the case in the American League Championship Series, game four would be pivotal. Up 2–1, the Blue Jays could take complete control of the series with a victory. But if Atlanta won, they would know that with two games left at home, they could win the championship by winning two out of three.

This time, though, the Series wouldn't turn on a dramatic comeback. Instead, it would be a pure pitching masterpiece by Toronto starter Jimmy Key, who had contributed precisely three innings of relief in the 1992 playoffs. Facing Atlanta first game starter and winner, Tom Glavine, Key worked his subtle magic, a game of finesse and control, all pitching and no throwing.

"Atlanta had good lefthanded hitting," Roberto says. "You always need a lefty, and Jimmy Key did a great job for us all year long. He had good control that day. He was throwing the ball on the corners, throwing it where he wanted to. When you have that control, it's going to be a good game. He's a groundball pitcher. He has to hit the corners. Throw inside and outside. He doesn't throw real hard, but he knows how to pitch. He knew how he was going to have to pitch to those guys. Whenever you have a guy like Jimmy Key out there, you have confidence in him."

It was Key's last start as a Blue Jay — he would leave for New York in the off-season as a free agent — and it was a wonderful way to say farewell to the fans who had been cheering him on since 1984. He took control in the first inning, picking off Otis Nixon after he had singled to lead off the game, and then cruised into the eighth inning, retiring twenty of the next twenty-one batters. His teammates hadn't provided him with much offensive support, since Glavine was also in top form — Borders homered in the third to put Toronto up 1–0, and Devon White made it 2–0, driving in Kelly Gruber with a single in the seventh.

In the eighth, though, Key finally ran out of gas. Gant led off with a double. Brian Hunter beat out a bunt, advancing Gant to third. Damon Berryhill, bunting for some reason, popped up, and then Mark Lemke hit a ball off the mound that Gruber barehanded and fired to first for the out. Still a run scored, and it was 2–1 with a runner in scoring position.

It was time for the old one-two: out came Key, to a standing ovation, and in came Duane Ward. He struck out Otis Nixon, who would have been the third out, except that the ball skipped by Pat Borders, and Nixon was safe at first. Ward then got the fourth out of the inning, coaxing Jeff Blauser into grounding to first, with Olerud making a nice play to finally end the inning.

In the top of the ninth, out went Ward, in came Tom Henke. Three hitters, eleven pitches, and the game was over. The Blue Jays won 2–1. They led the World Series three games to four. They could win it in Toronto the next night.

And guess who could be the hero? Jack Morris, the guy who had finished off the Braves a year before, and the guy who was 0 for the playoffs for the Blue Jays. It would be poetic justice, then, if in the ultimate big game, the ultimate big game pitcher got the win.

That was a possibility only until the fifth inning. The Braves had jumped to a 1–0 lead in the first when Otis Nixon doubled on the first pitch of the game, stole third, and then scored on Terry Pendleton's double. "Nixon's improved his game a lot," Roberto says. "He didn't used to be that good a hitter, and now he's a great hitter. He sprays the ball all over."

The Jays tied it in the second when the hot-hitting Borders doubled in Olerud, the Braves went up 2–1 in the fourth on a David Justice homer, and then Toronto tied it again in the bottom of the inning when Olerud singled and eventually scored on a single by Borders.

Then came the fifth and the One Big Mistake, the same thing that had plagued Morris throughout the playoffs. The Braves had already scratched out a run with two out when Nixon singled, stole second, and scored on a single by Deion Sanders. Then Terry Pendleton hit a ground-rule double, forcing Sanders to hold at third. Justice was walked intentionally to load the bases.

Through all of that, Gaston sat still as a statue, though many second-guessers in the crowd figured Morris had proven beyond doubt that he just didn't have it. Cito thought that he was still Toronto's best bet to pitch to Lonnie Smith, who was 1–10 in the Series. Morris got two quick strikes, then a ball, then he threw a fastball that didn't sink, that just sat there in the middle of the strike zone. Smith jumped all over it and sent it into the bullpen beyond the leftfield fence. The grand slam made it 7–2, and only the most cockeyed optimist didn't figure that the series was headed back to Atlanta. The Braves pitching combination of John Smoltz and Mike Stanton made sure of it.

"They went five runs up, and we knew that it was going to be tough to get it back, because they had great pitching," Roberto says. "We were disappointed, but that didn't mean we were going to lose yet. We didn't change our thinking until the end.

"But when the game was over, we started thinking about game six. That was the one we knew we had to win. We didn't want to have to play game seven."

12

 THE BEST

Everybody knows the equation. They had seen the World Series the year before, Jack Morris had seen it close up, and so there was little reason to feel cocky taking a 3–2 lead back to Atlanta, back to the chanting and the chopping, back to the other guys' town. The last five teams in Series history to return home down a game had rallied back to win the last two and the championship. Morris and his Minnesota Twins had turned the trick against Atlanta in 1991, with the Homerdome maniacs howling in the background.

If that was an intimidating place for visitors to play, then walking into Fulton County Stadium was like walking onto another planet. On a gorgeous, clear night of October 24, 1992, the sound seemed to swirl around the concrete oval, modulating only between loud and louder, and the hands and the headdresses and the tomahawks joined in a wave crashing again and again towards the field. Though baseball players, according to their unwritten code, are supposed to

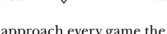

approach every game the same way, they approach this one differently. The scene, the situation, the stakes, all dictate that tonight will be a night like no other.

"The first five games of the series I felt nothing," Joe Carter says. "It was just like any other baseball game. And then in the sixth game, I had butterflies. I thought I must have been getting sick from some food I ate before the game. Finally I settled down."

"Nobody cared about game seven," Roberto says. "We wanted this game. This was the game we knew we had to win."

Steve Avery, the Braves starting pitcher, had performed well against the Blue Jays in game three, throwing eight strong innings and striking out nine. Then Alomar singled to lead off the ninth, and thanks to the generosity of the Braves bullpen, eventually scored the winning run. That had been the Jays' first exposure to the young lefty, and they had learned something vital from the experience.

"We knew we were going to run now because Avery has a real high kick and a slow motion to the plate," Roberto says. "All we have to do is get on base and put pressure on him."

Entering game six, Roberto is 2–18 for the series, and riding an 0–6 hitless streak. "They were good pitchers," he says. "You have to give credit to their pitchers. And the strike zone was a little bigger than what we expected it to be. There's nothing you can do with the umpires. But for some reason, in game six the strike zone was so small that you felt comfortable at the plate. That's why I felt better, because I knew that John Shulock, who was behind the plate, was one of the best umpires in baseball right now."

As the television broadcast comes on the air, the

Alomar family is tuning in from three distant corners of the hemisphere. In Salinas, Maria and Sandia are at home with friends in Monserrate watching in the living room. The whole town is watching somewhere, and by the time the game starts, the streets seem deserted, just as they will in Toronto. "The neighbours watched TV, everybody watched TV in this town," Maria says.

"Even in Guayama," says Carmen Pabon.

"Today is the day," Maria says to Sandia. "We win today."

"Don't say that," Sandia says. She is even more nervous than her mother, and that's saying something. "You never know."

Sandy Sr. is in Phoenix, in his hotel room near the Cubs minor league complex. His work keeps him from Atlanta, but of course nothing will keep him from the game this night. There are plenty of opportunities for companionship, plenty of places where he could watch the game surrounded by supportive friends. But instead, he sits in his room, alone. "I just wanted to watch it and relax," he says. "I wanted to watch it where I could pay attention to everything. I wanted to be laying in bed watching it and enjoying it. But it was too tense. It's funny. When you played the game, you usually don't get as tense as I did that time."

Near Cleveland, Sandy Jr. and his wife Christie are also a little tense, and not just because of the game that's about to begin. She is pregnant, she is full term, and as the game begins she senses that perhaps a force greater than baseball has taken over her body. But she doesn't tell Sandy. Not yet. She will grin and bear it because she wants to see Roberto win.

The game begins. Devon White leads off for Toronto with a single, and Roberto comes to the plate in a familiar situation. Devon will be trying to run, he will be hitting righthanded against Avery and trying to protect the runner early in the count. Then he will try to push the ball to the right side to move the runner along. The first run of the game is always important. Tonight it must be more important than ever before.

Devo makes it easy, stealing second with a huge jump. The throw from catcher Damon Berryhill isn't even close. "So then all I had to do was hit the ball to the right side. I didn't care if I got a hit. I just wanted the team to win. You just look for a pitch outside and try to hit it that way. If he pitches inside you don't swing. You can't try to do two things at once. If you're going to hit the ball to rightfield, you have to think that way. And if he throws it inside you have to just take it until you have two strikes, and then you change." After two balls, Roberto takes a strike on the inside corner. The next pitch is high and outside and he punches it towards the second baseman. He is out, but White is safe at third. "That's the way you win games. Now there's a man on third and all Joe has to do is get a flyball or something."

Carter steps up and hits a line drive to rightfield. David Justice seems to be in position to make the catch, but the ball glances off his glove. It is scored as a two-base error. White scores and Toronto leads 1–0. Carter is later stranded at third when Gruber grounds out.

In the bottom of the first, Toronto starter David Cone gives up a single to Terry Pendleton with two out before coaxing David Justice to pop up. In game two against the Braves, Cone hadn't been particularly effective, walking five in 4.1 innings, and was on the hook for the loss before Ed Sprague's memorable blast. As everyone reminds him, this game is the reason the Blue

Jays acquired him — it will be his last start in a Toronto uniform with free agency coming in the off season, and it will obviously be his most important. Time to pitch for a championship, and to add a few dollars to that enormous contract he'll sign with someone over the winter. It sure worked for Jack Morris.

Pat Borders singles to lead off the second for the Jays, continuing his remarkable series, but the Jays inning ends without any more damage being done when Cone hits into a double play.

In the bottom of the second, Cone pitches himself into trouble. He walks the leadoff man, Sid Bream. Jeff Blauser follows with a single to left. Berryhill hammers the ball to the warning track in centre, advancing Bream, and there are runners on first and third with one out. Lemke hits a short fly to centre that White catches. Bream tags, breaks for the plate, and then thinks better of it. Avery strikes out to end the inning. A runner on third, less than two outs and he doesn't score: in the middle of the season, that's how a hitter ends up paying a fine in kangaroo court. In the deciding game of the World Series, that's how your team winds up second best.

White strikes out to start the third, and then Roberto comes to the plate. He takes two fastballs inside for balls, and then a strike, an off-speed pitch on the outside corner. "He tried to throw the fastball and after that he tried to throw the change-up. He pitched backwards." The next pitch is another change-up that Roberto slaps into rightfield for a single, breaking his 0–7 drought. He steals second easily, his tenth in ten post-season attempts, advances to third on Carter's ground out, but is stranded when Winfield hits a flyball to right.

In the bottom of the third, with one out, Deion Sanders comes to the plate. The Two-Sport Wonder, antagonist of Tim McCarver, Neon Deion to the world, has been having a terrific series against the Blue Jays. He hits a hard groundball down the rightfield line that skips off Carter's glove. Carter is playing first because, with pitcher's hitting in the National League park in the World Series, Cito Gaston wants Dave Winfield's bat in the lineup. Winfield plays right, John Olerud sits out against a tough lefthander, Carter plays out of position and the Blue Jays lose a little defence in the process. Roberto runs into foul territory down the rightfield line to retrieve the ball and hold Sanders at second base.

With Terry Pendleton at the plate, Sanders steals third. As far as holding runners on is concerned, Cone is as vulnerable as Avery. Pendleton then hits a sacrifice fly to tie the game, and the choppers chop in ecstasy.

Hold that thought, because it isn't going to be tied for long. Candy Maldonado, the pride of Humacao, Puerto Rico, leads off the fourth with a home run into the seats in left, and it is 2–1. "That put us ahead and put pressure on them again. Avery was struggling with his control a little bit. He was falling behind a lot of batters." The Blue Jays go for the kill against Avery. With one out, Pat Borders doubles down the leftfield line, and Atlanta manager Bobby Cox gets Pete Smith up in the bullpen. The hook comes out quickly in a game like this. Avery strikes out Manuel Lee, but then walks Cone on four pitches. White follows with a single to left that Sanders charges hard. Borders, chugging around third, isn't much of a runner and Sanders' throw comes fast and reasonably accurate, just a little bit in front of the plate. Berryhill fields the ball, blocks the plate beautifully with his left shin pad, and tags

Borders out. Borders never even reaches the plate.

Sid Bream flies out to begin the bottom of the fourth inning, and Jeff Blauser steps up.

Blauser hits a groundball hard up the middle. Roberto picks up the ball off the bat, gets a quick jump, takes four strides to his right and then launches his body into the air. He is fully extended, his glove hand stabbing forward, his body a foot off the ground. He snares the ball on the second bounce while in mid-air, lands, turns on his knees, and throws to first while in the process of popping up. Blauser is out. It is a series of movements worthy of a gymnast, an amazing feat of co-ordination, one for the highlight films, a play that will be always associated with this series.

In the broadcast booth, the normally verbose and eloquent Tim McCarver is reduced to saying: "Oh man, what a play."

"I never thought I had a chance to make the play," Roberto says. "I thought the ball was going to go through. That's a quick field in Atlanta. If the ball goes through, it could have been a long inning. Who knows?" Instead, after that, the Braves are done on a Berryhill strikeout.

"I've seen some plays that Robbie's made that were better than that," Sandy Sr. says. "I remember seeing Robbie make two plays against Montreal when we were in San Diego. They gave me goosebumps. One was against Tim Raines and one was against Delino DeShields — back to back. Both were backhand plays going towards the bag. One of them he threw from his knees. The other one was one of those where he's running, he slides, he pops up and throws. Raines was surprised he was thrown out. He said in the paper the next day that Robbie was the best."

"That's just Robbie," Cito Gaston says. "He makes play after play like that all the time. You get spoiled watching him because he might do that two or three times a week."

With Pete Smith pitching, Roberto grounds out to second to lead off the fifth inning. Carter follows with a double, but he is stranded after Nixon makes a nice running catch on Winfield's line drive to centre and then Maldonado makes the final out. The Braves come to bat and again, their failure to execute costs them a run. Mark Lemke walks to start the inning. But the pitcher, Smith, can't put down a sacrifice bunt, a skill they drill from the first day of spring training, and one that any National League pitcher ought to have mastered. He ends up fouling off his final bunt attempt with two strikes for a strikeout. So when, one out later, Deion Sanders singles up the middle, Lemke stands at third instead of tying the game. He doesn't get any further because Cone strikes out Terry Pendleton swinging on a 3–2 pitch to end the inning.

Neither team does damage in the sixth, though Manuel Lee's single keeps a streak alive — Toronto has recorded at least one hit in each inning, a trend that will continue for the first nine. The Braves go down in order in their half.

In the seventh, Roberto hits an infield single into the hole between short and third with one out. He is off and running again, but Carter fouls off the pitch, likely depriving Alomar of the chance to tie the major league record of eleven consecutive successful steals in the post-season. Carter goes down when Terry Pendleton makes a great play on his hard shot to third, and Winfield flies out to end the inning.

David Cone has done his job. In his final appearance

as a Blue Jay, he goes six innings, gives up one run on four hits, and leaves with his team just nine outs away from victory in what could be the deciding game of the World Series. Cito Gaston, who has benefitted all year from having an extremely deep bullpen, has that and more at his disposal this night, since everyone but Jack Morris and Juan Guzman are ready and willing to go. First out is Todd Stottlemyre, normally Toronto's fourth starter. He strikes out Lemke, induces a ground out from pinch hitter Jeff Treadway, and then allows a single by Otis Nixon.

Now come some of the decisions that make or break a manager's reputation. Deion Sanders is due up, and he has been to the Blue Jays what Pat Borders has been to the Braves. He has two hits and two stolen bases on the night, eight hits in the series. The combination of him at the plate and the speedy Nixon on the basepaths spells trouble for Toronto, even with two out. Nixon has stolen five bases in the Series without being caught — he wasn't caught by Pittsburgh in the National League Championship Series either — and Pat Borders and the pitchers have been having a terrible time with opposing baserunners throughout the playoffs, allowing sixteen stolen bases against Oakland and fifteen so far against Atlanta.

So Gaston makes a move — out goes the righthander Stottlemyre, in comes the lefthander David Wells to neutralize the lefthand hitting Sanders and to help neutralize the runner at first with his above-average pick-off move.

Over in the Braves dugout, Bobby Cox has a tough decision to make. Do you manage by the book and lift your best hitter for a righthander? Or do you leave Deion in and take your chances? Deion, who hit .310

against righties, averaged a more than respectable .271 against lefties during the regular season, including a double, four triples, two home runs and five RBIs in just thirty-six at-bats.

Cox opts for baseball orthodoxy. Out of the game goes Sanders, in comes Ron Gant, who has hit .254 against lefties during the season, but has also driven in 32 runs in 88 plate appearances. He hasn't done much of anything in the Series.

It turns out that it isn't the batter-pitcher part of the match-up that matters (although as the game goes into extra innings, Cox might not have minded having Sanders in the lineup). The difference is in the running game. Wells holds Nixon close, preventing him from getting a good jump. When he finally tries to steal, Borders makes a quick accurate throw that Roberto takes at the bag, sweeping down a tag that catches Nixon on the top of his batting helmet. Score one for Cito. There are six outs to go.

In Salinas, in Cleveland, in Phoenix, and of course in the SkyDome, where the Toronto faithful have gathered en masse to watch the game on the Jumbotron, there is a sense that this time it's for real. The Jays have reached the eighth inning one run up, and they still have their all-but-unhittable tandem, Duane Ward and Tom Henke, waiting in the bullpen. So many times during the season, that had meant game over.

Maldonado's single is all the Jays can come up with in their half of the eighth against reliever Mike Stanton. It is Ward who walks to the mound to face the Braves in the bottom of the inning. So far during the series, he has pitched 2.1 innings and surrendered just one hit. The first batter he faces is Gant, who was left at the plate when Nixon was caught stealing. Gant rips a line drive towards the gap in right-centre. Dave Winfield sprints towards the ball.

Winfield's fielding abilities had been an issue before he ever came to Toronto. Originally, the Jays braintrust expressed no interest in signing him as a free agent because they understood that he would insist on playing the outfield, and they needed only a designated hitter. That was resolved though, with Winfield deciding that being a designated hitter on a potential championship team would suit him just fine. He played occasionally in the field to spell the regulars, but it wasn't until the World Series in the National League park against a lefthander that Gaston had to really count on him. In the eighth inning of a 2–1 game, the hordes of armchair Gaston-bashers back in Toronto were no doubt wondering why Carter hadn't been moved from first to right, and Olerud from the bench to first. If there was ever an excuse for defensive substitutions, this was it.

In private during the season, Winfield maintained that he could play the field just as well as the guys who were doing it regularly for Toronto. He is not one moved to false humility, especially when it comes to his own athletic talents. This night, he proves it, running, sliding, fighting the lights and making the catch, depriving Gant of extra bases.

"We won that game with defence," Roberto says. "There were a lot of good defensive plays. I made one, Dave Winfield made one that would have cost a run. That's why sometimes I get upset because people talk about hitting, hitting, hitting. Well, hitting is just one part of the game. You have to talk about good defence too. You win more games with the glove than with the bat."

Ward strikes out Terry Pendleton. He walks David Justice. Then Sid Bream hits a harmless flyball to right. There are three outs to go and Henke is ready in the bullpen.

The Jays seem anxious to get the game over with in the top of the ninth. White and Roberto swing at first pitches and make first pitch outs. Carter doubles down the line to left — for some reason, Pendleton the third baseman isn't guarding the line late in the game — and Cox brings in hard throwing reliever Mark Wohlers. He gets Winfield to ground out to short.

When Roberto Alomar was a little boy, he used to pretend that he was playing in the biggest game there was. "He said, One day, mom, I'll be there," Maria remembers. "He was dreaming all the time. He said, I dream that I bat a home run. All the time." And at some point in those dreams it was the bottom of the ninth in the deciding game of the World Series, and he was standing on the field, watching the play in front of him, waiting for the moment when the players would run to the pitcher's mound and jump together in joy and know that, at that instant, they were the best in all the world.

Here it is the bottom of the ninth, and here he is, twenty-four years old, five years in the big leagues and on the verge of something his father was never lucky enough to experience. This team will never be the same as it was at this moment: Tom Henke, Candy Maldonado, Joe Carter, they will all be free agents at season's end. So will David Cone, so will Manuel Lee. Other players, great players, could spend half a lifetime in the game and never get this far. In twenty years, Dave Winfield has only been there once, and he lost. This will be a moment to savour, just as it will be for the fans of

Toronto, who had their hearts broken so many times, just as it will be for his family and friends and for the entire town of Salinas and the entire island of Puerto Rico. Three outs and it is theirs.

Henke is on the mound, and he has been untouched in the World Series: two innings, no hits, two saves. During the regular season, he had blown just three saves in thirty-seven opportunities and the Blue Jay bullpen as a whole has gone seventy-seven games without letting a lead fritter away in the late innings. That said, the Terminator isn't the intimidating presence that he once was. There was a time when he could throw mostly heat, could just ride his fastball up through the strike zone, finally getting batters to whiff at something travelling 95 mph at eye level. These days, he is more likely to change speeds with his forkball, to spot the fastball, to finesse hitters rather than simply overpowering them. But whatever he has been doing, it worked, and aside from Dennis Eckersley (Remember him? Remember what happened to him?) there is hardly a more consistent closer in the game.

Jeff Blauser leads off. He shoots a single between second and third. Gruber is guarding the line, as he should be, and can't get to the ball. The crowd erupts. The leadoff man is on. Up comes catcher Damon Berryhill — the man responsible for the game-winning homer in game one. But he won't be swinging for the fences in this situation. This demands a sacrifice bunt, something Berryhill has accomplished just seven times in his five major league seasons, and not at all in 1992. But he gets it down, not perfectly but well enough. It rolls in front of the plate to Henke, and he has no choice but to throw to first. The tying run is in scoring position.

Lonnie Smith, the man who hit the grand slam in game five, is up next, pinch hitting for Lemke. They are still chopping and chanting in the stands, but they're also praying — really — with heads bowed and hands clasped, pleading with the God who deals with baseball games. Ted Turner and Jane Fonda are standing, and on the bench some caps are already turned backwards, the mystical gesture said to spur a rally. There is some precedent for their hopes — ten days ago, in game seven of the National League Championship Series, in the bottom of the ninth with two out, the Braves had snatched victory on a pinch hit single by obscure back-up catcher Francisco Cabrera. The play had been immortalized on signs and t-shirts everywhere in Atlanta. And if it happened once . . .

Smith takes a strike, then another. Then two balls. He fouls one off. A third ball. Full count. Another foul. And then ball four. The chanting gets louder, the chopping more emphatic, more caps are turned. Guts start to churn wherever the Blue Jays are beloved.

Hitting for the pitcher is . . . Francisco Cabrera. Once the property of the Jays, soon to be the answer to a trivia question, a guy who makes a paltry $140,000 a year in a game of millionaires, and who supports a wife and two kids and his parents and brothers and sisters back home in the Dominican Republic. Now, he can be doubly sainted in Georgia.

Cabrera has a fine at-bat, fouling three pitches off with the count 2–2. Henke then hangs one out over the plate and Cabrera extends his arms and meets it with the fat part of his bat. The ball sails on a line to left-field. Maldonado takes two steps in, and then realizes that perhaps he's misjudged the speed and distance on this one. He hustles back a couple of steps then leaps high, pushing his glove to the heavens. If he misses, if the ball goes by him to the fence, the Braves win and it's on to game seven. In the infield, Manuel Lee leaps with him, in empathy. Maldonado just makes the catch, the ball just wedges in the mesh of his glove.

Now the Jays are just one out away, and all of that praying, all of that mock-Indian stuff hasn't made a lick of difference. Only Otis Nixon stands between Toronto and the championship. At first base and second base, a couple of fellows are feeling extremely confident that this will indeed be the final out of the year.

"We told Henk, he's killing us if you pitch him outside," Carter says. "Robbie and I knew Nixon from playing in the National League. We told Henk, just bust him inside with fastballs. He can't handle them."

And, temporarily, Henk heeds their advice. "The first pitch he threw him was an inside fastball, and he swung for strike one," Carter says. Two strikes from the championship. "The second pitch, he took a fastball inside for strike two." The Blue Jays are one strike away from winning the World Series, when Henke or Borders or both of them has a different notion. "On 0–2, he threw a forkball out over the plate and he hit a single. Robbie and I just said to each other, Oh God, doesn't anybody listen?"

The ball is hit into very shallow leftfield, where Maldonado scoops it up with Blauser just two strides past third base. There will be a play at the plate — or there would be, if Maldonado didn't throw the ball high into the screen. The score is 2–2. The clocks in the east are striking midnight, and this thing isn't over after all.

In Salinas, groaning is heard all over town. "I was very nervous," Sandia says. "That was terrible. I don't want to remember."

In Phoenix, hotel guests in at least one establishment hear a sudden loud thump. "When the game got tied in the ninth inning, I hit the wall," Sandy Sr. says. "I hit my fist in the wall."

In Cleveland, there is plenty of pain and it isn't just psychological. "Christie was holding out there for awhile, it was amazing," Sandy Jr. says. "She was there watching the game and she was in pain but she didn't want to tell anybody. Well, I guess she did say something, but we didn't really want to pay attention. She said, 'Aw, I'm hurting,' but she always says she's hurting so we really didn't pay too much attention. We said, 'Shut up, Winfield's batting now.' I told her to relax, use the Lamaze, breathe hard. Then Henke was pitching and they tied and everybody went, 'Oh, my God.' It's a wonder that she didn't have the baby right there."

"It was a terrible feeling," Roberto says. "But, hey, we were playing in their stadium. If they came back in this game we would have had to play game seven. That would have been a lot of pressure. If Candy had made a good throw, he would have got him. All we had to do was get the next guy out and play another inning. We didn't want to disappoint the fans again. We had to win game six. We didn't want to play game seven in their stadium." There are runners on second and third with Ron Gant at the plate. And in *their* stadium, they know theirs is the team of destiny, they know that any club that has twice come back from the brink must be special. They know their prayers are being answered.

Gant works Henke to a full count, swinging for his second strike at what looks like ball four. Then Henke throws the forkball low and Gant goes and gets it, and it looks for a second like he got it good. "When Gant hit that ball, I wasn't sure when it came off the bat that it was staying in the ballpark," Carter says. "But I saw Devo put his hands up and then I said, that's that. Let's go get some more runs."

The tenth inning decides nothing. Veteran Charlie Leibrandt comes in to pitch for the Braves. He has been a starter all year, and a reasonably effective one, but given the Braves bullpen woes, he's a good bet in relief at this point in the game — a lot better bet than Jeff Reardon, anyway. He gives up a single to Gruber, but strikes out pinch hitter Pat Tabler, batting in Lee's spot, to end the inning.

Henke stays in to pitch for the Jays, a very rare occurrence, since he's been a one-inning man all season. He gets Pendleton to ground to first and Justice to ground to short, where Alfredo Griffin makes a nice play to retire him. "He helped a lot of people this year," Roberto says. "He helped Manuel Lee. Alfredo is a veteran, and people listen to him." With lefthander Sid Bream coming up, Gaston heads for the mound. Out goes Henke, in comes Jimmy Key, the hero of game four. "That was a great move," Roberto says. "It showed he was thinking about winning that game. He wasn't thinking about game seven." Key retires Bream on a ground out, and it's on to eleven.

Cox decides to stick with Leibrandt, though he has the cursed Reardon warming in the bullpen. With one out, Leibrandt hits Devon White in the thigh. White doesn't try awfully hard to get out of the way, but it counts, and the go-ahead run is on base. Roberto comes to the plate.

"I've seen Charlie Leibrandt before, so it's easier for me. He throws a lot of change-ups, so I was just trying to not let him fool me. I was trying to use my hands. If you're thinking change-up, you have to look for a change-up you can hit good. I was trying to go to right-field. I had that hole open with the man on first. If he threw me a ball inside, I'd just let it go. I wasn't using my stride a lot, or my legs — just my hands. I was just trying to stay back and let my hands do all the work. Sometimes if you use your body too much or your legs too much with a guy that doesn't throw too hard, you start to kind of open up and pull off the ball. If you stay back, you're going to stay more on the ball.

"He threw me a change but he left it a little bit up in the zone. If he had thrown the change-up a little lower, he might have got a groundball for a double play. But he threw the pitch up high, and those are the kind of pitches you're going to hit good."

Roberto lines the pitch into centrefield for a single. White holds at second. Carter is up. Reardon is ready, Cox is thinking about it, but he's probably also thinking about those awful moments earlier in the series. Leibrandt stays in the game and gets a harmless flyball to centre from Carter. There are two out, and Dave Winfield is the batter.

He hasn't had as horrible a World Series as the one he had in 1981 — that would be tough to duplicate — but still, he has driven in only one run against Atlanta and he doesn't have an extra base hit. He works Leibrandt to a 3–2 count, and then comes the moment that all Jays devotees will tell their grandchildren about. He smacks the ball hard down the leftfield line, past Pendleton, who is shading towards the hole. Alomar scores, White scores, it is 4–2 Blue Jays and again they are three outs from victory.

Key is still pitching, and the Atlanta fans, who have been riding a roller coaster throughout these playoffs, are sitting in the valley hoping to climb one more peak

— even though the odds are very much against them. But you've gotta believe, don't you? Blauser singles to left. Berryhill hits what ought to be a perfect double play grounder to Griffin, but it kicks up on a bad hop and goes by him. Berryhill is on first and Blauser gets around to third and there is still nobody out. Jane Fonda is looking heavenward and absolutely everyone is chopping and even the Blue Jays biggest boosters are feeling that bad old feeling again: 1987, Chet Lemon, the ball just clearing the wall at Tiger Stadium. Spare us, Lord, another trial like that one.

Rafael Belliard pinch hits and does his job perfectly: the sacrifice bunt moves the all-important runner from first base into scoring position. Brian Hunter, a powerful first baseman who hits a lot of home runs off lefties, follows. Cito sticks with Key. Belliard grounds out to first, a run scores, Berryhill advances to third, but there are two out.

Guess who's coming to bat?

It had been a wonderful series for Otis Nixon even before his bottom-of-the-ninth heroics. His speed and his smarts at the plate have served the Braves well. He is a switch hitter who hits lefthanders a lot better than righthanders. But hitting from the left side, he is also a step closer to first base. On an infield groundball, on a chopper in front of the plate, on a bunt — and he has been known to bunt for a hit with two outs — he'll have a better chance of beating it out. Beating it out now means a tie game.

Gaston heads for the mound. Key is the best pitcher he has available at the moment, but he decides that he wants Nixon batting lefthanded. In comes Mike Timlin, a twenty-six-year-old in his second big league season. His previous brush with Blue Jay history wasn't a pleasant one.

In game three of the 1991 American League Championship Series, he and his manager had shared the goat horns: Gaston for bringing him in instead of Tom Henke to start the tenth inning, and Timlin for giving up what turned out to be Mike Pagliarulo's game-winning homer in the pivotal game of the series. In 1992, he didn't pitch until June 13 because he was recovering from off-season elbow surgery. His numbers overall weren't that impressive, but in September, when it counted most, he was marvellous. Still, for Gaston to go to him in this situation represents an enormous vote of confidence, and will give the Cito-haters plenty of ammo should things not turn out well.

"He asked Jimmy Key and Key said it was better to bring in a guy like Timlin," Roberto says. "In game four, Nixon hit well against Key. Timlin has one of the greatest arms on the team. He's got a great sinker. He throws a real heavy ball. And he's got a great slider. Pitchers are not machines. They're going to get hurt and they have to work hard to come back. That's what he did. He didn't moan about it. He had to go to the minor leagues, he had to go through rehab and he did all that. He came back and did a great job. I had real confidence in him. Nobody thought that it would be him that would come in and save that game. I was real happy for him."

Again, the Toronto Blue Jays are one out away from a world championship. Again, for Roberto and his teammates all of those little boy dreams come to the fore. Again, for the fans the nightmares of the distant past — and of the bottom of the ninth past — are very much a part of the mix; high excitement and dread rolled together, the feeling almost unbearable. In the movies, every game ends like this. In the real world, you could spend a lifetime watching the home team and never experience this once, never mind twice in one game. This time, though, it's for real, the defining moment for the fans and the franchise.

Nixon steps in. He is swinging on the first pitch and fouls it off. "I was looking for the bunt. I was moving ahead, because if it goes by the pitcher, it is my play." On the second pitch, Nixon is bunting, trying to drag the ball past the pitcher along the first-base line. It doesn't go far enough: Timlin fields the ball cleanly, then turns and throws to Carter, who has scurried over to cover the bag. "It wasn't an easy play. Because he's got a great sinker, it was hard to bunt, and the ball didn't go that far. Still, he had to go there and make a good throw. He threw nice and easy. Sometimes you go in a hurry and you throw the ball away." The play is close, but not that close. Out says the umpire. The Blue Jays don't have to wait for the call. They are swarming the pitcher's mound, jumping on each other, hugging and yelling and crying, probably, with Roberto in the middle of it all.

"We felt real proud about what had happened," Roberto says. "We reached a goal that every player wants to reach. Now when we retire, we can say that one time we were the World Champions."

There was enough pride to spread around.

In Toronto, the crowd in the SkyDome erupted, and soon the streets were filled with celebrants. Across Canada, people joined in toasting a sports victory as they hadn't since that ill-fated night in 1988 when Ben Johnson won his tainted victory in the Seoul Olympics.

In Phoenix, a man not prone to wild outbursts of emotion or bouts of excess sentimentality allowed himself a little whoop of joy. "I knew how much it meant to him," Sandy Sr. says. "As soon as it was over, I called over to Puerto Rico right away. I talked to Robbie later that night."

In Salinas, the victory party started right away. "Everybody jumped in their cars and were blowing their horns, fifty, sixty, seventy cars," Luis Rosa says. "They call them caravans. The whole town went wild. Roberto has become a hero to the people of Puerto Rico."

"We had many friends here," Sandia says. "They love Robbie. The game finished so late — at one o'clock in the morning, but everybody stayed awake to see it. Then everybody came here. It was a wonderful experience."

"The cars were going 'Hoooo, Hoooo,'" Maria says. "Everybody was coming here and saying congratulations. The people came here, the kids, they all celebrated."

"We didn't sleep," Carmen Pabon says. "We stayed up 'til morning. Everybody got out of their houses and came in their cars, like a parade. Blowing the horns, and screaming and jumping in the streets, and singing just like they were singing over there."

In the dressing room and at the hotel, the Blue Jay celebrations continue long into the morning, and in the middle of them an old guy comes up to a young guy and tells him how he feels. "It was great to have a person like Dave Winfield come up to me and say, 'Roberto, you're one of the best players I've ever seen.' A guy has been in the big leagues for twenty years and he says that. He's played with a lot of people. Saying that to me was like being Santa Claus. He was real happy. He came through in the last inning and hit the double. He said you don't know what a World Series means until you win one. He waited twenty years. There are a lot of people who've never been to one. I'm only twenty-four and I feel proud because I've been in three All Star Games, I won the silver slugger, I've won two gold gloves, and now I've won the World Series. It was a great feeling. I didn't sleep much that night."

No one was sleeping much in Cleveland, either. "When the game was over, Christie said, 'Well you know, Sandy, I think I'm really going into labour now.' I said, 'Why didn't you tell me?' She said, 'I wanted to watch the game and I wanted to watch Robbie celebrate.' She stayed to watch the celebration, and then we went to the hospital."

At 5:41 that morning, Marissa Alomar is born.

 EPILOGUE

Returning to Toronto after the World Series, Roberto was as euphoric as any of the Blue Jay fans. "I've seen him happy and I've seen him sad," says Betty John. "After the World Series, that was the happiest I've ever seen him. That was the pinnacle for him. And now that he's tasted it, he wants it again."

"The parade was great," Roberto says. "There were a lot of people there. I never thought there were going to be that many people. It was real emotional for me talking in front of all of those people and getting the big ovation. Being with your fans and all your team-mates — some of them for the last time — it was fantastic. I knew there were going to be a lot of free agents on the team, so you have to enjoy it while you can. After that, I stayed in Toronto for awhile and spent some time with my friends."

The demand for personal appearances and auto-graph sessions had never been greater. Roberto remained in Toronto for nearly two months after the season ended, considering endorsement offers, going to one event after another, and at the same time coming down from what had been the longest baseball season of his life.

Early on it became clear that the championship team of 1992 would never be reassembled. The economics of baseball dictated that even a rich franchise like Toronto couldn't afford to pay all of its free agents the kind of salaries they would demand on the open market. Instead, Pat Gillick, President Paul Beeston and the rest of the front office would have to pick and choose, keeping some players, letting others go, and making moves to fill the vacancies. By the time they were done, the Jays would look very different than they had that last night in Atlanta.

Gone, to no one's surprise, was David Cone, signing with his hometown Kansas City Royals. Gone was Tom Henke, signing with the Texas Rangers, the team where he had begun his major league career, after the Jays decided that the younger Duane Ward was ready to become their full-time closer. Gone was shortstop Manuel Lee, also off to Texas, with no real replacement on the horizon for Toronto. Gone was Kelly Gruber, traded to the California Angels. He would later surprise his new employers by having surgery on his shoulder just before spring training for an injury he said he suffered during the World Series. Neither the Jays nor the Angels apparently knew anything about it, and for a time there was talk that California might try and have the trade ruled null and void, though they eventually relented. Gone was Jimmy Key, a World Series hero and a Blue Jay for his entire professional baseball life, off to the New York Yankees. Gone was Candy Maldonado, who signed with the Chicago Cubs, and Dave Stieb, who would try to resurrect his career with the Chicago White Sox.

And, most surprisingly, gone was Dave Winfield. It had seemed at the end of the season that Winfield's re-signing with Toronto for 1993 and beyond would be a mere formality. Instead, Gillick and Winfield's agent reached an impasse, and the Blue Jays decided to go in another direction entirely, signing free agent Paul Molitor, who had played his entire career with the Milwaukee Brewers. Molitor didn't have Winfield's power, but he hit for a higher average, was a base-stealing threat, could play occasionally in the infield or outfield, and he was younger.

Still, a lot of Blue Jay fans were heartbroken over the departure of someone who had been so important to the franchise during his single season in Toronto, and one eccentric local politician even tried to set up a fund whereby Torontonians could help defray the costs of signing Winfield. Eventually, after a farewell press conference in Toronto, Winfield signed with the Minnesota Twins, returning, like David Cone, to his hometown.

Along with Molitor, the Jays made some other important acquisitions. They signed Dave Stewart, the Oakland As pitcher who had been so brilliant in the American League Championship Series. Veteran short-stop Dick Schofield, who was coming off shoulder surgery, was given the chance to compete with Eddie Zosky for the starting job vacated by Lee. Utility infielder Luis Sojo came over in the Gruber deal, and Darnell Coles, another utility player who can do time both in the infield and outfield, was signed as a free agent.

Most importantly, the Blue Jays re-signed Joe Carter,

who had tested the free agent market. He was actually offered more money by Kansas City, but said that he felt comfortable and right coming back to the Toronto organization.

Roberto watched the winter's goings-on and wondered just what kind of team he would be part of by the time spring training rolled around.

"I knew Cone was going — to Kansas City or some other place, maybe Philadelphia," he says. "I was surprised that they didn't sign Jimmy Key — but I'm not a general manager. That's a lot of money he's being paid in New York. Toronto has a budget and they can't spend so much money. Everybody asks me about Manny Lee being gone. All I can say is that I just go out there and do my job. If I do my job and the shortstops do their job, it's going to be fine. I don't have to worry about that. Manny was a really good shortstop. I felt real comfortable with him. Sometimes you have to make some changes, and they did.

"I think Wardo can be a real good closer. And Stewart is a great acquisition. It's going to be a good pitching staff again. I was disappointed about Winfield because he was a great guy for us. He was a great guy to have around, a great hitter. But Molitor is a great hitter, too. It's two different players, Winfield and Molitor. We still have a great lineup, but it's going to be different.

"I thought all along that the first priority was to sign Joe Carter. I knew he was going to come back here. They treated him good and he's part of the franchise. He's a guy who has 100 RBIs every year. A guy who hits 30 home runs. A guy you enjoy playing with. A guy who puts emotion in the game, a guy who pushes everybody. He can do a lot of things. So signing him had to be their first choice. I was real happy when he signed.

"I know it's going to be a different team this year, different people, different guys, but we still have a good team. We're still the team to beat. We're just going to go out there and have some fun and play the game. We'll just have to see how we come together. You have to put the World Series behind your back. It's over already. You have to look forward to this season. I want to win. I don't care if we've won five World Series or ten. I still want to win."

Roberto's own opportunity to test the free market won't come for another three years. Given his age and the fact that he is widely regarded as one of the best all-around players in the game, he would surely be able to command an enormous salary somewhere.

But right now, he thinks that he'd like to stay in Toronto for as long as possible. A lot has changed since the chilly day he first arrived in town (and then fled soon afterwards) after being traded from San Diego. This is his second home now, a place where he has been made to feel very welcome, and where his talents are appreciated by capacity crowds, game in and game out. And it is an organization that is committed to putting a winning team on the field every season. That combination, he realizes, would be hard to top.

"Toronto is beautiful," he says. "My first impression was that it was too cold, but now, one of these days, I'd love to spend a Christmas there. I've never seen Christmas snow.

"I'm just waiting to see what's going to happen to me in three years, when my contract is up. If they give me another long-term contract, I would buy a place to live in Toronto and make my home there. I like Toronto. People treat me real nice. You can go anywhere and they recognize you. I never knew it would be that way.

You cannot ask for more. And I love Canada. I'm not just saying that because I play baseball there. I like the fact that there's less crime in Canada. You can go out and have fun in any place. In Puerto Rico, you have to be careful.

"In Toronto I can go out and talk to the people and give autographs to people. I always say yes, because I know baseball is not going to be forever."